In Pursuit of Excellence

How to Win in Sport and Life Through Mental Training

Second Edition

Terry Orlick, PhD

Leisure Press
Champaign, Illinois

Library of Congress Cataloging-in-Publication Data

Orlick, Terry.
    In pursuit of excellence : how to win in sport and life through
    mental training / by Terry Orlick. – 2nd ed.
        p.   cm.
    Includes bibliographical references.
    ISBN 0-88011-380-4
    1. Sports–Psychological aspects.   I. Title.
    GV706.4.O73   1990
    796'.01–dc20   89-39657
                                                                          CIP

ISBN: 0-88011-380-4

The quotes highlighted on the first page of the following chapters are attributable to the author: 1, 3, 8, 11, 13, 15, 18, 21.

About the cover: The medal on the cover is an actual gold medal awarded to Harold Osborn, winner of the decathlon and high jump at the 1924 Olympic games in Paris. (Courtesy of Mrs. Harold Osborn.)

Developmental Editor: Peggy Rupert, MA; Assistant Editor: Timothy Ryan; Copyeditor: Jean Tucker; Proofreader: Linda Siegel; Indexer: Barbara Cohen; Production Director: Ernie Noa; Typesetter: Sandra Meier; Text Design: Keith Blomberg; Text Layout: Denise Lowry; Cover Design: Hunter Graphics; Cover Photo: Wilmer Zehr; Back Cover Photo: Anouk; Interior Photos: Athlete Information Bureau/Canadian Olympic Association; Printer: United Graphics

Printed in the United States of America   15   14   13   12   11   10

Leisure Press
A Division of Human Kinetics
Web site: http: // www.humankinetics.com/

United States: Human Kinetics, P.O. Box 5076, Champaign, IL 61825-5076
1-800-747-4457

Canada: Human Kinetics, Box 24040, Windsor, ON N8Y 4Y9
1-800-465-7301 (in Canada only)

Europe: Human Kinetics, P.O. Box IW14, Leeds LS16 6TR, United Kingdom
(44) 1132 781708

Australia: Human Kinetics, 57A Price Avenue, Lower Mitcham, South Australia 5062
(08) 277 1555

New Zealand: Human Kinetics, P.O. Box 105-231, Auckland 1
(09) 523 3462

To my mother, for the greatest gift—unconditional love and support. And, to my father, for letting me steal his great ideas.

Contents

□

Acknowledgments

I am continually indebted to the athletes, coaches, and students with whom I have worked, who have allowed me to learn and grow as they have explored their own potential.

I am also sincerely appreciative of John Bales of the Coaching Association of Canada, who has continued to support me and my work, and Nadeane McCaffrey, who was of great assistance in the revisions for this second edition.

Without the persistence of Rainer Martens I probably never would have proceeded with a second edition of *In Pursuit of Excellence*. Thanks are also extended to Peggy Rupert for her editorial assistance and Damon Burton, who offered excellent comments in his review of my revised manuscript.

□

Preface

Getting Ready

If we don't change, we don't grow. If we don't grow, we are not really living. Growth demands a temporary surrender of security. It may mean a giving up of familiar but limiting patterns, safe but unrewarding work, values no longer believed in, relationships that have lost their meaning. As Dostoevsky put it, "taking a new step, uttering a new word, is what people fear most." The real fear should be of the opposite course.
Gail Sheehy

Intense involvement in sport as a competitor, coach, and mental training consultant has given me a multidimensional perspective on excellence. The most valuable lessons I have learned about pursuing excellence and coping with the stresses of high-level performance have come from my personal experiences with athletes. Some have been world champions; others have been in pursuit of a better world. All have been dedicated to improving their own level of performance and to exploring their own potential.

I'm always excited when I work or talk with people who really commit themselves to perfecting their mental skills because they are the ones who make the greatest advancements, physically and mentally. They are the ones who open new doors. They are the ones who leave their pursuits having learned the most valuable lessons. There have been individuals like this on each team with which I have worked, and it has been a joy to interact with them. It's exciting to watch them take charge of their own lives and to witness their amazing growth as performers and as people. We are all capable of this kind of growth when we open ourselves to developing our mental strengths.

Tapping into your own potential and achieving your own goals requires an individualized approach that will allow you to fully develop your mental and physical strengths.

The most valuable lessons in life come through opening yourself to experiences that teach you about living, loving, coping, and pursuing your dreams. Sport is one endeavor that provides this opportunity. Athletes who take the mental game seriously leave their sport carrying with them what is ultimately most important of all: skills for living a higher quality of life.

This is the first of my dozen or so books that I have reread critically for the purpose of updating and improving. It has been a very interesting experience.

I have completely rewritten the original *In Pursuit of Excellence*, drawing upon 10 years of additional experience with athletes in the field. New examples have been added to almost every chapter that clearly communicate how athletes have effectively implemented various strategies in pursuing their goals. Entirely new sections or chapters have been written on relevant, applied sportpsych topics such as elements of excellence, "feeling" imagery, focusing, relaxing through exertion, and distraction control. I know a lot more than I did when I originally wrote *In Pursuit of Excellence*, and that new knowledge is reflected in this edition. Overall, it is a much more solid and insightful look at excellence than the first edition.

The most effective strategies and approaches followed during my individual consultations over the past 15 years are outlined in these pages. I have tried to provide clear guidelines and enough specific examples to allow you to assess your own situation and come up with your own self-directed program for excellence.

This edition is divided into three parts, each of which includes chapters that reflect a specific theme. Part I, Realizing Your Potential, focuses on helping you recognize your inner strengths. Part II, Paths to Excellence, offers various techniques to make the most of your mental and physical resources. Finally, Part III, Overcoming Obstacles, provides strategies and advice to help you through the trying situations that we all face from time to time.

The whole process of revitalizing this book made me realize how much I've learned during the past 10 years, working and talking with so many great athletes and coaches. I'm thankful for having been given so many rich learning opportunities. The overall high quality of experience has been consistent with virtually every group of athletes with whom I have worked, from alpine skiers and figure skaters to basketball players and canoeists. Within this book I share their mental strengths and some of the strategies they used to successfully overcome the obstacles they faced.

When the best aspects of many unique experiences are combined, there is an incredible reserve of strength and scope to be drawn from. If some of the most creative and effective approaches utilized by our best performers today can be learned and integrated into our lives, we all have something to gain—not only on the fields of sport but also on the paths of life. We can attain higher levels of personal excellence and greater life satisfaction by living some of the approaches outlined in this book. This is precisely why it was written and revised.

Part I

Realizing Your Potential

Preceding page: Elizabeth Manley, silver medalist, figure skating, 1988 Olympics, Calgary.

Chapter 1

□

Personal Meaning

We want not only to live but to have something to live for. For some people this means to pursue excellence through sport.

Exploring Our Limits

My personal experiences as a competitive athlete have been rich ones, bringing memorable highs that remain with me. Some involved achieving personal goals; others involved close human relationships; still others involved the sheer joy of being absorbed in the experience. I reached one of my achievement highs when I first did a quadruple twisting back somersault on the trampoline. Some people were impressed. Others might say, "So what? Who cares if you can spin your body in the air four times before landing? What difference does it make?"

It may not make any difference to anyone else, but it made a difference to me. It felt great to accomplish something that required a commitment to extending my personal limits. Over a period of about 8 years, it began to happen bit by bit . . . half twist . . . full . . . double . . . triple . . . three and a half . . . three and three quarters . . . quadruple! I remember an excitement rushing through my body . . . a satisfaction at having explored my potential in one small, seemingly meaningless but personally meaningful, area of existence. I had stretched my personal limits.

The desire to do your personal best, to excel, to attain the highest standards of performance, to be supreme in your chosen field is a worthy human ambition, which can lead to increasingly high standards, personal growth, and personal meaning. If none of us were concerned with the quality of our contributions, our work, our creations, products, or services, our society would take a marked turn for the worse. Yet high levels of achievement and the pursuit of excellence in any field do not come easily. The trail is hard and steep. There are numerous obstacles to overcome and barriers to push aside. Becoming a highly skilled person in any field—sport, art, medicine, science, writing, teaching, or parenting—demands commitment and sacrifice.

3

The greatest barriers in our pursuit of excellence are psychological barriers that we impose upon ourselves, sometimes unknowingly. My failure to even attempt a quintuple somersault is a good example. Somehow I had come to believe that it was impossible. Perhaps it was like the 4-minute mile. At one time that too was viewed as an impossible barrier . . . until it was broken by one man . . . and then almost immediately by a host of others. It wasn't the physical makeup of runners that changed; it was their belief in what was possible. As your beliefs about limits change, the limits themselves change.

While traveling through Southeast Asia I had the opportunity to see barefoot men walking across hot beds of coal. Those glowing embers generated incredible heat, yet the walkers emerged unblistered and unscarred. Is this unbelievable feat within the capacity of normal human beings? How many of us will ever call upon this capacity? How many of us even believe that it is possible? Therein lie our limits. The firewalkers are made of the same flesh and blood as you and I; it is their belief that is different. Therein lies their strength. Belief gives birth to reality.

Exploring Ourselves

Since I retired from active competition, my personal sport-related highs have come primarily through outdoor experiences . . . running, canoeing, cross-country skiing. I have never formally trained or competed in these activities, yet they offer an abundance of meaningful experiences.

One winter night, the sky was clear, the moon was full, the night air crisp. The snow sparkled like dancing crystals under the moonlight. It was a majestic evening as we set out to ski up the mountain trail to a small log chalet nestled among the trees. At the chalet we made a fire, had some wine and a bit of stew, and joked a little; then we headed back down the mountain. As I skied down I became one with the mountain, not knowing where it ended and where I started. I was so close to it, hugging it and feeling it hug me, as I flowed along that narrow snow-packed trail. I moved into shadows and out of shadows as the moonlight darted through the trees. I was totally absorbed in the experience. It was novel, challenging, sensual, fun, exciting, physically demanding—a meaningful trip with nature . . . a peak experience, the kind that makes it great to be alive.

Sport provides ample opportunity to free ourselves for short periods to enjoy pleasure and excitement not readily available elsewhere in society. In sport we can live out our quest for excitement, personal control, or risk by deliberately accepting challenges that we then attempt to meet. We like to feel competent and capable of directing our own lives; this is one of the reasons we seek out challenges both within and outside of sport. Great satisfaction comes from the actual experience of becoming competent and feeling in control.

The continual process of seeking out and meeting challenges that are within our capacity (not too easy but not totally out of reach either) is the heart of human motivation. People are looking for "delicious uncertainty," challenges that present a difficulty but that also are potentially within control. What is delicious for me may not be for you. We each seek our own level.

As a white-water canoeist I discovered that the challenge of running a river is not a conflict between human and nature, it is a melding together of the two. You do not conquer a river, you experience it. The calculated risk, the momentary sense of meaning, and the intensity of the experience let you emerge exhilarated and somehow better. It is a quest for self-fulfillment rather than a quest for victory over others or over the river. Many sports can be viewed in the same way. Each experience or exploration can lead to enlightenment and discovery. There is no way to fail to experience the experience, and experiencing becomes the goal. The experience may lead to improved performance, self-discovery, personal satisfaction, and greater awareness, or it may simply be interesting in its own right.

This became clear while I paddled down the legendary South Nahanni River in the Canadian Northwest Territories. No one else can ever totally understand what that river meant to me. So it is with the river of sport and life. No two people perceive things in the same way, even at the same instant. Each view is unique, each experience separate, each course different and irreplaceable . . . and so it should be.

Answering life's challenges in our own way is what provides personal meaning for each of us. A failure to respond to those challenges leads to hopeless abandonment in the prime of life. In many prisoner-of-war camps, those who lacked the awareness of a meaning worth living for abandoned their will to live and curled up and died. Those who knew that a task or purpose awaited them survived the most incredible horrors and hardships. Suffering ceased to be suffering the moment it found meaning. Viktor Frankl (1968), a young doctor who survived the horrors of imprisonment in a death camp, discovered through his experience that "striving to find meaning in one's life is the primary motivational force in man" (p. 154). It literally made the difference between life and death.

Although meaning for each of us is unique and subject to change, it seems to flow most readily when we are striving toward some goal that we find worthy or feel is worthy of us. We can experience meaning by committing ourselves to certain goals, ideals, or values; by experiencing someone or something of value to us; by creating something; by choosing to do something for others, with others, or by ourselves that we deem worthwhile. Sport is a wonderful medium for providing a sense of purpose and a sense of continuous challenge, as well as a range of intensity and emotion that is difficult to experience elsewhere. It can be a rich and meaningful encounter if we approach it on our own terms. There are few contexts where we have such close contact with other people, with nature, and with ourselves as we have in sport. Sport offers numerous opportunities for personal growth and for stretching the limits of human potential, both physically and psychologically.

Personal excellence is a contest with yourself to draw on the natural reserves within your own mind and body, to develop your capabilities to the utmost. The true challenge lies in personal growth, enjoying the pursuit of your goals and in living the various areas of your life.

Each of us begins at a different departure point, mentally, physically, and with respect to the support we are given. Make the best of the talents you've been given and the situations that you face—no matter how limited or unlimited they may be. Your quest for personal excellence requires making the most of what you have—whatever that may be.

Chapter 2

Commitment and Excellence

**My greatest power in life is my power to choose.
I am the final authority over me. I make me.**

A year and a half before the 1984 Olympic Games, diver Sylvie Bernier decided that she was going to win the Olympics. As the Games approached she often dreamed about achieving her goal, "like flashes all the time. Every day I would see myself walking down and getting the medal. When it actually happened, it felt like I had already done it before."

For 18 months before the Olympics, Linda Thom wrote in her diary every single night, "I am the 1984 Olympic Gold medalist in Ladies Match Pistol," and it came true. She imagined herself on the podium having won, the flag going up, the anthem being played, reporters interviewing her, all of these things. Somewhere deep in Linda's core was a belief that she could do it. Thinking about her daily goals and dreaming her dream nourished her determination, her confidence, and her belief in herself as a champion.

Two weeks before skating at the 1988 Winter Olympics, silver medalist Elizabeth Manley had a vivid dream of skating her long program in the Olympic Saddledome. She skated a perfect program. Tears of joy and relief streamed down her face as she stood at center ice waving to the capacity crowd as it rose to its feet. She woke up crying with joy, her body in a sweat. The dream was real: As it turned out, she lived that dream 2 weeks later, with a beautiful long program at the Olympics.

All three of these athletes were extremely talented, highly motivated, and had great people support; they also had a dream. Each great human accomplishment begins with some kind of vision or dream. Every great feat flashes in the mind before it surfaces as concrete reality, whether it be flying to the moon, creating a better society, healing oneself, pursuing a relationship, building a bridge, or climbing a mountain. Dreams precede reality; they nourish it, perhaps even create it.

Most often our dreams of excellence are reflected as visions of our hopes and aspirations, or as images of things we want to do or places we want to go. They may flash in our mind during waking hours while we are walking, running, or cycling, or during quiet times when we are alone with our thoughts. Dreams of excellence, of creative accomplishment, of harmonious relationships are in themselves stimulating and fun; they provide a lift even if they do not always become absolute reality.

All the people with whom I have worked who have excelled at anything began with a dream of being their best, of making a contribution, of pushing their limits, or of reaching the top. Think about your own dreams; let them flash through your mind, often. Go after your dreams; let them lead you. It's the only chance you have to move along your path of excellence.

Psychological Separators

Why is it that two runners with identical physical capacities (percentage of fast- and slow-twitch muscle fiber, reaction time, limb size, aerobic capacity, etc.) run vastly different times? One becomes a world champion and the other a mediocre runner. Why do some athletes with all the right physical attributes never really excel? How do athletes with relatively little going for them physically meet world-class standards in extremely demanding events? The answer lies in using what one has to the fullest capacity.

Excellence is housed in a variety of shapes, sizes, colors, and cultures. Many great athletes emerge from highly systematic programs, but others come from countries that lack a real sports system. Personal excellence is largely a question of believing in your own capabilities and fully committing yourself to your own development.

When my colleague Dr. Al Reed and I were studying components of excellence for a talent identification project, we started by interviewing some of the world's best athletes, coaches, and scouts to get their views on the ingredients necessary to "make it" to the highest level in their sport.

Within each sport there was disagreement about the physical attributes necessary for excellence but almost total agreement on the psychological attributes. Commitment and self-control were seen as the keys to excellence. To excel in any field you must be committed, and you also must develop enough self-control to perform well under a variety of potentially stress-producing circumstances.

To excel in anything—a sport, a relationship, or a business—you must begin with commitment. At some point you have to say, Hey, I want to be really good at this; I want this to work; I am going to do everything I can to be as good as I can be; I am making this a priority in my life.

To be your best, you must live this commitment and regularly stretch what you perceive to be your current limits. Commitment alone doesn't guarantee success, but a lack of commitment guarantees that you'll fall short of your potential.

Olympic champion paddler Larry Cain and all-American basketball player Misty Thomas are living examples of the kind of commitment required to become the best that one can be. They are two of the most committed athletes with whom I have ever worked. Their commitment is reflected in the incredible intensity they bring to practice and competition. When they train they are there for a reason—to do their best and to accomplish their goals, every second out there. In competition they are supercharged and superfocused. Nothing less than their best effort is enough. Their minds are on the right channel, and they are determined to do their best—no matter what.

Personal Commitment

Your personal level of commitment is something you must work out for yourself. No one can tell you how important something is in your life; that is your decision. But it is clear that people who excel are extremely committed people. There is no way to achieve a high level of excellence without a high level of personal commitment.

At this point it might be useful for you to rate the importance of excelling in sport, or in another pursuit, on a scale from 1 to 10. A rating of 10 indicates that it is the most important thing in your life (high commitment), a 1 indicates it is not very important at all (low commitment), and a 5 indicates a middle position between the two.

How important is it for you to excel in your sport (or other pursuit)?

1	2	3	4	5	6	7	8	9	10
Not very important							The most important thing in my life		

When a large group of marathon runners responded to this commitment scale, it became evident that those with the highest commitment (i.e., scores of 9 and 10) became the fastest runners. As the commitment score decreased, the performance level decreased proportionally. The same was true for athletes in a variety of other sports.

When members of the Swedish national badminton team were asked what was the main difference between them and others who did not make the national team, their response was commitment (for example, "wanting it more," "being willing to train harder and longer"). Their best athletes were those who were already most committed as juniors. They stayed after practice and watched others play, they practiced more or with more concentration, they did "the extra," they were willing to make sacrifices, and they believed that they would one day be excellent players. Support and encouragement from loved ones, families, or coaches often enhanced their commitment.

In a study with the National Hockey League, we interviewed top NHL coaches and scouts to learn what they saw as most important for a player to make it in the pros. We asked them what they looked for when drafting a junior player and why they thought that some players who were selected didn't make it. Desire, determination, attitude, heart, and self-motivation were most often mentioned as the crucial ingredients that tilted the balance between making it and not making it at the professional level. Giving the hockey career top priority, maintaining personal pride, constantly trying to improve, and always investing maximum effort were named as indicators of the kind of commitment necessary to succeed. The chief scout for one of the NHL's top teams expressed it as follows:

> The main thing is that the player is willing to give that little extra when it's needed. . . . He's preparing himself to give that little bit more . . . even when he might be dead tired. . . . This separates the good hockey player from the great hockey player.

Why Athletes Don't Make It

In the NHL study physically talented athletes who did not make it in the major leagues were found either to be lacking in the area of commitment or to be unable to cope with the stress of the pro situation, on or off the ice (for example, "could not cope with pro demands," "choked under pressure"). The difference between making it and not making it was highlighted in a discussion of the drafting of one of the NHL's most celebrated players—Bobby Clarke, former team captain and then general manager of the Philadelphia Flyers hockey club.

> We drafted Bobby Clarke on our second round, but there was a boy we drafted on our first round who was bigger and stronger, could skate and shoot better than Clarke, but Clarke made it and he didn't. He never had the heart for the game. He wasn't willing to sacrifice that little bit extra that you need to be a professional hockey player. In practice Clarke would be there 10 minutes longer and he would

work harder. In a game he got himself mentally prepared to give the extra . . . the other player didn't do that. Result—one went ahead, the other fell behind. Clarke did extra work on the ice, where he had to give a little more to check the man, where he had to bear down. Where it showed more than anyplace is coming back. . . . Gotta give a little more. If you lose possession of the puck, now you have to dig down to your bootstraps for extra adrenalin to come back and check the man. Bobby Clarke would always show that. The other boy would put his head down and sort of give up. That's the difference between the two.

A commitment to do the work is a prerequisite for excellence, but unless you also master the art of self-control you will continue to fall short of your dreams. Excellence requires the development of good focusing skills, as well as an element of openness to the input of others.

A well-respected NHL coach who guided his team to a Stanley Cup Championship and to victory over the Soviet Union offered some interesting advice in this regard:

- *Accept Criticism.* "Our superstars can handle constructive criticism. . . . They can even handle unfair criticism. . . . If they make a mistake, they acknowledge it and do everything in their power to not make it again. . . . A person with star potential will not become a star if, when I criticize him or point out a mistake, he tries to fight me."
- *Don't Be Afraid to Fail.* "If a superstar ever sees a slight opening, zip, he has the courage to go for the small hole. He won't hold back because he's afraid to fail."
- *Maintain Composure.* "The best players maintain their composure . . . when there's a call that goes against them, maybe even a bad call. They stay cool, look to correct, and try to calm down the other players."

Elements of Excellence

My personal experience consulting with Olympic athletes through four Olympic Games and numerous world championships has taught me that most athletes fail to perform to potential in important competitions for the following reasons:

- They are not well enough practiced at overcoming distractions.
- They are not well enough practiced at focusing totally on their task for the entire performance.

- They have not done enough quality imagery, quality training, and competition simulation to refine the mental and physical skills required to excel in competition.
- They are not well rested when it is time to compete.

PREREQUISITES FOR EXCELLENCE
(As Viewed by NHL Coaches and Scouts)

- Does constant work on the ice; is in on the action, always after the puck, the check, or the goal; makes things happen; gives a little extra when it is important.
- After a mistake, goal against, or coach's criticism, comes back with a strong shift, makes the right moves, stays in the play or game, and tries harder to correct or make up for the mistake.
- Never gives up (for example, takes a check, gets back into the play quickly, tries and tries again).
- Plans, evaluates, and corrects with linemates on the bench; encourages others; passes to better-positioned players on the ice.
- Takes tips, asks questions, listens, admits errors and corrects them without excuses; shows that he wants to learn.
- Pursues activities both in and out of season to maintain conditioning and improve skills (for example, fitness training, power skating).
- Learns to perform in a big game as well as in a normal game; comes through in tight situations or close games; makes the big play when needed.
- Learns to stay motivated, come back, and play well after a setback, mistake, missed chance, call against himself or team, or bad penalty.
- Learns to control temper (for example, does not needlessly retaliate after a hit or setback).
- Learns to react to referee, coach, teammates, and fans in a mature and positive way, particularly in big games.
- Learns to adapt to the stress of success, travel, and playing with different players (for example, line switching) without negative effects on attitude or play.
- Learns to stay cool and confident under pressure (for example, is not moody and not a worrier; can maintain concentration on getting the job done in pressure situations).

If you are serious about becoming the best you can possibly be, the most essential ingredient is your commitment—to do the right things. It takes an incredible commitment to reach the top: a commitment to train and rest your body so that you can perform under the most demanding conditions and a commitment to train your mind to focus totally on executing your best performance skills under the most stressful circumstances.

If you really want to excel, the following basic guidelines will help immensely:

- Set specific daily goals so that you know what you want to accomplish every day and every training session.
- Before training, take some time to prepare mentally, so that you get the most out of yourself during each training session.
- Commit yourself to executing your skills in training with the highest quality of effort.
- In training, simulate what you want to do or have to do in competition. Run through complete, clean routines, programs, plays, or events on a regular basis.
- During scrimmages, run-throughs, and time trials, commit yourself to focusing 100 percent, every step of the way. Be totally connected to your task.
- Do imagery every day to prepare yourself to accomplish your goals. Imagine yourself achieving your goals and successfully executing the skills you are trying to perfect.
- Approach your performance imagery as an experience involving all of your senses. Try to call up the feelings of the moves. Experience your performance the way you would actually like it to occur.
- Quality imagery is a way of programming your mind and body to perform more closely to perfection on a consistent basis.
- Gaining quality and control of your imagery is a learning process that takes time. Be persistent. It will lead to a higher level of concentration and an overall improvement in your performance.
- When preparing for an important competition, rest well, listen to your body, and avoid overtraining so that you remain strong and healthy. The commitment to rest well is as important as the commitment to train hard. Without proper rest, the mind-body system falters and eventually shuts down.
- Know what focus works bests for you. Where is your focus when you perform best? Respect this focus. Remind yourself to follow it in training simulations and in competitions.
- Practice overcoming distractions on a daily basis for high-quality training, better competitions, and happier living. Avoid wasting energy

on things beyond your control, and commit yourself to remaining positive.

- Before important events, remind yourself of the focus that works best for you. Follow the pre-event preparation patterns that have resulted in your best performances. Imagine and feel yourself executing your perfect performance. This will ensure that the best performance program is fresh in your mind and body. Then close off your thinking and connect totally to your performance. Turn on your autopilot and go.
- Draw the lessons out of every competition. What went well? What needs refining? Were you able to hold your best focus for the whole event? What do you want to do in the same way next time? What changes might be helpful? How do you want to approach your next competition? What reminders might help? Make a note of these points and work on them so that you are even better prepared, mentally and physically, for your next challenge.

Chapter 3

□

Focusing

Where the mind goes, everything follows.

One night I was driving down a little dirt road in the countryside near my home. Something darted out of the darkness onto the road in front of me. My heart pounded as I lurched for the brakes. A large rust-colored cat was in pursuit of a little gray field mouse. The cat focused on that mouse as if nothing else in the world existed, as if some kind of radiant energy beam connected the cat to the mouse. If I had not hit the brakes I would have run over the cat—but she pursued that mouse as if I didn't exist. Only after she had the mouse firmly clenched in her teeth did she acknowledge my existence before sauntering off into the woods. This is an example of focusing—the uninterrupted connection between two things: a cat and a mouse, a performer and his performance, an athlete and her goal.

Did you ever observe a young child at play? I'm sometimes amazed at children's ability to focus. When I watch a 3-year-old friend playing, I swear that, while he plays, the only thing that exists in his world is the movement of his little red truck. He is oblivious to the chaos around him. His connection is very similar to the connection of the cat and the mouse on the road. If a little kid and a cat can focus so completely, why can't we?

Let's suppose that the cat began to worry about being judged on her form as she stalked the mouse: Do you think the complete connection would remain? If, while my 3-year-old friend were playing, he began to worry about being assessed on his truck-maneuvering ability by all the big people around him, do you think the flow would be broken?

A 14-year-old competitive figure skater came to see me a few years ago precisely because she had lost this connection. She had entered her first major competition when she was 11 years old. At that time, she just went out and let it happen. She skated in the same way that my little friend played with his truck, totally absorbed in her performance and oblivious to the outside world. It was only later, when she started to think about judges, other skaters, the audience, and evaluation, that she started getting uptight. "When people said I was expected to win, the feeling of pressure started." Her thoughts began to drift to others' expectations of her. She began to worry about her performance and about how it would affect her acceptance by others. That is when her anxiety began to rise and her performance began to slide. That is when she lost her focus—her natural connection.

As she attempted to regain this connection, what worked best for her was to try to recreate the focus and feelings that she had taken into her sport in her earlier years, to focus only on her own performance and forget about everything else.

When you free yourself from dwelling on outside pressures or expectations, when you know that you will continue to be a valuable human being regardless of numerical outcomes, worry is less likely to intrude and disrupt your performance or your life. This is when your focus is free to flow naturally. Worry is one of the greatest inhibitors of skilled performance. If you can learn to view competition in a less worried way, or if you can find a way of focusing that is more absorbing than the worry, you will be well on your way to consistent performance at your optimum level.

Focusing in Sport

When you are focused in sport you are aware of only those things that are critical to your performance, to the exclusion of everything else. In a very real sense you and your performance become one, and nothing else in the world exists for that period of time.

In individual sports, best performances occur when athletes are totally connected or riveted to their performance, often to the point of performing on autopilot and letting their bodies lead . . . without interference. In team sports best performances likewise occur when players are totally focused and absorbed in the crucial aspects of their performance. They are totally aware of the flow of relevant play around them, completely trusting in their capacity to automatically read and react to that awareness, and totally connected to the execution of their own moves. Their focus must be readily adaptable like the zoom lens on a camera, capable of zooming in and zooming out. For example, a point guard in basketball or a quarterback in football needs a wide-angle perspective when focused on reading the field for an open receiver, then a zooming in on the open player and an inner awareness of making a crisp and accurate pass. The ideal performance focus is total connection to your performance even though the demands of the performance may be constantly changing.

It is important for you to discover what focus works best for you and under what specific circumstances. Initially you may experience it for only short periods. Work on allowing this focus to become a natural part of all of your performances.

Your best focus may initially feel like a nonfocus because often you are letting a performance program unfold automatically—free from conscious thoughts, directives, or self-evaluation. Often it just means tuning into your body, or being aware of the key feelings that accompany your moves when they are executed flawlessly. A lot of focusing practice in sport involves learning to stay connected to what you are doing, to your body and its feelings; not letting irrelevant or distracting thoughts interfere with the natural performance program in your mind and body; trusting your body to do what it's been trained to do without forcing; and directing your body when it begins to tire or deviate from an efficient performance program.

To improve your focusing skills and make them more consistent, set some goals to allow your best focus to surface more regularly. Here are seven practice tips that will help.

1. In training, feel yourself execute a skill, program, or play in your mind and body through imagery; then do the skill, letting it unfold naturally—thought free.
2. When you practice skills, focus on being totally connected to your moves.
3. If your sport requires an awareness of other players or opponents to whom you must react, practice being aware of everything that is going on around you, then totally connect to your target.
4. In training and competition allow yourself to execute your own moves and to react to the moves of others without evaluation. Just let it go and see what happens. Go by feel. Go by instinct. Free yourself to flow naturally.
5. Try to recreate the mental and physical conditions that allow you to experience the feelings and focus associated with your best performances.
6. Use reminders to enter the state of mind that allows your best performance focus.
7. Work on holding that focus for short periods, and try to gradually increase the time you are fully focused. The ultimate goal is to be able to hold that best focus, that total connection, throughout your entire performance—every move, every step, or every stroke of the way.

Hitting Your Target

The goal of a world-class archer is to hit the center of the target with each arrow shot. He trains himself to find the middle of the middle, to see only one center.

> In this state of full concentration he could be anywhere in the world and distractors would be eliminated. He shoots each arrow as a separate achievement concentrating fully for the short period required to fire that shot. The periods between should always be relaxation periods where all tension, muscular and mental, is dissipated and the mind freed from the last arrow in preparation for the next one-arrow effort. (R. Genge, 1976, p. 2)

One world champion archer described focusing as "blocking out everything in my world, except me and my target. The bow becomes an extension of me. All attention is focused on lining up my pin (sight) with the center of the target. At this point in time, that is all I see, hear, or feel. With the bow drawn and sight on target, a quick body scan can tell me if anything is 'off.' If everything feels right, I hold focus and simply let the arrow fly. It will find the target. If something feels off I lower the bow and draw again."

Once a person has trained his muscles and nervous system to shoot an arrow into the middle of a target, theoretically he should be able to put it into the center every time. What prevents him from doing this? Fatigue? Sometimes—but not on the first few rounds. Wind? Sometimes—but not on a calm day. What then? Like most other athletes, archers are prevented from achieving total accuracy by worry, by distracting thoughts, by overactivation, by a loss of focus, or by a lack of connection with the target. They have the program in their brain to perform the skill flawlessly. They can do it without thinking. Their challenge, like yours, is to free the body and mind to connect totally with the goal.

What the world's best archers and shooters seek, and must perfect, is a relaxed focus. It's not that the focus itself is relaxed, in the sense of lacking intensity. It's rather that the mind is cleared of irrelevant thoughts, the body is cleared of irrelevant tensions, and the focus is centered only on what is important at that moment for executing the skill to perfection. The body is relaxed but ready, and the mind calm but focused. Outside thoughts and unwanted tension are absent. The focus is centered on a specific target. The target may be the image of the perfect move, a total connection with one's own body, or the center of the target that is waiting to receive the shot. Relaxed focusing often follows a sequence, from mind (mental imagery) to body, from target to performance. Each step eliminates nonessentials so that the single focus or vision can fully absorb the performer's awareness. Developing an ability to direct focus to critical performance cues and hold it there until the body is free to follow the visions of the mind is crucial to high-level performance.

Relaxed focusing is a learned skill that must be practiced to be perfected. Here are some general exercises, involving both relaxation and focusing, that you can try:

- Sit quietly, let yourself relax, and focus on looking at something like a blade of grass, an insect, a flower, a painting, a piece of fruit, a leaf, the bark of a tree, a friend's hand or face, a cloud. Really focus on it; look closely at its unique design; get absorbed in it.
- Sit quietly, let yourself relax, and focus on listening to something like the voices of birds, the wind, the leaves, or other sounds that you hear around you. Get absorbed in one of those sounds; then let it fade away by absorbing yourself in another sound or another focus.
- Line up several targets or objects. Become aware of all the targets. Then begin to narrow your focus until you are aware of only one target, then the center of that target, then the center of the center of the target. Let all other visions blur into the background; let all external sounds become inaudible. Connect with that target.
- Focus on a specific thought (or target), then let your thoughts wander, then refocus on the specific thought or target.
- Stand quietly, let yourself relax, and think about a particular skill. Imagine and feel its perfect execution in proper sequence and timing (for example, position, form, style, technique). Then empty your mind, and let your body perform that skill automatically.
- Before executing a skill, take a moment to relax and repeat the thought or image upon which you wish to focus (for example, center, center, center; form, form, form; stretch, stretch, stretch; reach, reach, reach; power, power, power). Then execute the skill.
- Seek the feel of the movement. If the feel is right, the arrow will find the target. (The same concept applies to various moves or skills.)
- When you are feeling stressed, see what happens when you slow everything down. . . . Talk slowly, move slowly, stretch slowly, focus on breathing in a slow, deep, and relaxed way.
- When you are distracted, practice clearing the distractions from your mind by zeroing in on what you have to do to perform effectively. Everything else is unimportant, unproductive, nonessential.
- After an error, immediately shift your focus to what will help you execute the next skill correctly. Practice this.

- Practice relaxed focusing with other people watching (for example, while you are reading, pounding nails, chopping wood, or doing sport skills). Relax, then focus.
- Practice shifting your concentration back and forth from your body to your target.
- Prepare yourself to focus on one shot, one stroke, one swing, one skill at a time, disregarding past and future. Remind yourself of this focus every day.
- Use simple reminders or cue words (for example, focus, smooth, relax, let go, tough defense) to keep your mind on target. Have a cue word that will zap you into your best focus.
- Enjoy your performance.

If you experience problems with focusing, try to let it happen easily without forcing it. Liken your efforts to this ancient Chinese saying: "Sitting quietly, doing nothing, spring comes, the grass grows by itself."

The world's top athletes achieve their best results when they focus only on their performance and not on the outcome. This focus is reflected clearly by the following top athlete: "For my best performances I'm thinking about how to shoot correctly (form); letting shooting sequences run through my head . . . seeing myself in control, confident. It is very important for me not to start adding the score and projecting what the score might be. If during the last few ends I become nervous and start to worry about blowing it, I have to work hard to keep my shooting sequence in mind (form, form, form) and not the glory of shooting a high score."

Another top Olympic athlete maintains, "I'm not nervous in a negative sense in advance. I remain who I am, myself, so that it is impossible for other competitors to have a harmful effect on me." She doesn't go through a big comparison scene, worrying about how well others are performing. She simply does her own thing. "For my best performances, I empty my mind and I feel as though it isn't me performing, but at the same time I feel totally connected with the feelings in my body. It's as if my subconscious is doing the performance. I imagine the perfect movement in my head and the rest follows automatically." After the event she evaluates why her performance was good or bad. If it was good she asks herself, How did I get my mind working that way, so I can duplicate it the next time? If her performance was not up to par, she draws out the lessons and moves on. "I probably work harder and learn more when something goes wrong."

The difference between best and worst performances lies within your thoughts and focus. In worst performances you allow negative, anxiety-producing, or distracting thoughts (about other performers, your inadequacies, others' expectations, the amount of rest, a bad warm-up, the weather, or final placing) to interfere with an effective task focus. In best performances you are able to stay in the moment, which is the only one that you can influence anyway.

If you find yourself losing your best focus, these strategies may help you regain it.

FOCUSING STRATEGIES

- Return to basics; follow your prepracticed game plan.
- Focus only on your target or immediate goal.
- Reassure yourself that you have trained and are ready (for example, I have done this skill a thousand times before—I am fully capable of doing it well).
- Remind yourself of your past best performances and recall the feelings and focus associated with them.
- Remember that your goals are realistic—all you want to do is to perform as you are capable of performing.
- Focus on doing what is right for you rather than worrying about what is wrong.
- Imagine the perfect execution of your skills, then do what you are fully capable of doing.
- Remind yourself to stay in the moment. Forget the past, the other athletes, the final score. Focus on doing your job.
- Intensify your focus on form.
- Remind yourself that it's just another game or performance.
- Do a careful postcompetition analysis of good and bad performances. It is invaluable, even 2 or 3 days afterwards.
- Training and competition should be enjoyed. If you hate it, leave it.

Why Worry?

Worry raises anxiety, drains energy, and diminishes your performance focus. Anything that shifts your focus away from worry can be helpful. Many athletes, once they are actively involved in the actions of the game, no longer feel anxious. This is because they have successfully shifted their attention away from worry or self-doubt to their bodily sensations or to an absorbing performance focus.

You can learn to shift your focus away from worry by focusing on something interesting, beautiful, or enjoyable or by completely absorbing yourself in executing your task. If your focus is centered on something other than worry, you cannot also be worrying at the same time. You can focus on the skill you are doing, the specific technique to be followed, the game strategy, positive imagery, your breathing—or anything else that does not involve evaluating yourself or putting yourself down. This shift in focus will help you avoid comparing yourself, doubting yourself, or worrying about distractions, possible failure, or the opinions of others. The goal is to remove yourself from the picture and to pay attention to the details of executing the specific task or to something unrelated to evaluation or outcome.

When attempting to shift focus, instead of trying to force yourself to concentrate on something, let your focus absorb itself in what you want to do next. For example, let your focus shift from self-condemnation over the last skill you performed to preparation for absorption in the next skill. If you practice this often in training and in competition, you will increase your awareness and effectiveness. You can practice shifting your focus of attention in a variety of settings. Scan the page that is in front of you now. Pick the last three words in this sentence and *focus on them*. Focus on these words until they stand out more than anything else on the page. Then back up your focus and let it roam so that you become aware of the whole page. Now pick the word *focus*, and let yourself become more aware of it than others around it. Good!

See how it feels to focus on different kinds of feelings, thoughts, or cue words in training. Have a run today and as you extend your leg, think *str-e-tch* or *float*. Do this about 10 times in a row. See what happens. Then try thinking *grab* or *power* when your left foot hits the ground and again when your right foot touches the ground. Do this about 10 times in a row. See what happens.

Do some body scans. Become aware of the sensations in different parts of your body. How do the soles of your feet feel right now as you sit here reading? Where is the feeling centered? Are your calves relaxed? How do the soles of your feet feel when you are walking or running? Find out.

What does your behind feel like right now? Tune into that feeling. Is it relaxed? Is it warm? Is there a feeling of pressure? Lift up one cheek, then the other. Does that feel better? I thought it might. Do it again. Become aware of your shoulders. Are they relaxed? Let them drop a little. Think relaxation into your shoulders. Wiggle them a bit. Roll your head. Relax. That's better. You're supposed to enjoy the simple pleasures in life.

Before reading the next chapter, close your eyes for a minute and let everything relax . . . let go. When you open your eyes, get up, stretch, and feel refreshed, so that you can really focus on what you are about to read in the next chapter, or on whatever you plan to do next.

Chapter 4

□

Personal Goals

A journey of a thousand miles begins with a single step.

I've had discouraged athletes and students come to me and say that they can't seem to meet their goals. The discussion usually goes something like this:

Me: *Did you set specific goals for yourself?*

Student: *Oh, yes—I tried it and it didn't work, so I stopped setting goals.*

Me: *What were your goals?*

Student: *To compete in the Olympics; To finish my thesis by the summer; To get an A in your class.*

Me: *Oh, I see. Do you have any short-term goals that are totally within your control . . . like what you are going to do today that will bring you one step closer to being your best?*

Student: *No.*

Me: *What about tomorrow?*

Student: *No.*

It's not unusual for people to set only long-term, far-off goals without focusing enough energy on the present. It is the present that gets you to the future in the manner in which you wish to get there. Long-term goals can help with motivation, but you also need lots of little *daily* goals that take you progressively to your desired destination.

When pursuing personal excellence it is best to focus your energy on specific aspects of performance that are potentially within your control—your skills, your preparation, your execution, your routines, your time, the best you can do that day. Avoid focusing on outcome goals that are beyond your immediate control, such as scores, placing, or winning. Generally outcomes are not within your direct control because you do not control competitors, teammates, judges, officials, playing conditions, or the weather—all of which influence outcomes. When you set goals that re-quire control over elements that are beyond your control, you set your-self up for frustration and needless anxiety. It is challenging enough to focus on controlling yourself and your own performance.

Daily Goals

For goal setting to be effective, establish specific daily goals, then encourage yourself, compliment yourself, and reward yourself as you achieve short-term goals and move toward long-term ones. You want to get from point A to point B as quickly and efficiently as possible, and this process helps you to get there. Let's say that you want to become the best athlete you can be, or that you want to write a book. Great! What are you going to do about it in the next 5 minutes, hour, day, week, month, year? Setting specific goals and pursuing them in a systematic way separates those who want to meet challenges and excel from those who actually do.

Let's take the writing of this book as an example. I could simply write as often as I feel like it and finish whenever, or if ever, the book is com-plete. Or I could set some concrete goals for myself, saying that I want to finish this section today, before eating supper; write the following sec-tion by the end of the week; finish the next chapter by the end of the month; complete the book by the end of the summer. I've tried the "do it when I feel like it" approach, and it never seems to advance me very far toward my goal. But when I set very specific short-term and long-term goals for myself, things begin to happen.

For me the process goes something like this. First, I think about whether completing the book is important to me. This is a critical first step be-cause only if I am committed to the goal do I have a realistic chance of achieving it. I decide that this goal is an important one because I like writing, creating, and reflecting, and I want to share my thoughts with others in hopes of helping them to achieve some of their goals. Sharing and help-ing others makes me feel worthy. Also, I love to see a bunch of thoughts become a bunch of roughly typed pages and then become a real live book. It's very concrete: I can see what I'm accomplishing, much as in sport.

The concreteness of progress in most sports is readily obvious. New tricks, better technique, faster times, higher jumps, better plays, improved rankings—all can be seen and felt. You know exactly where you are, and you can see progress in a way that is often not possible in other aspects of life. When I teach a class, for example, it is very difficult to know whether I've really accomplished anything. I'm not left with anything concrete that tells me where I am, where the students are, or whether I have effected any real change. Sport, on the other hand, offers indisputable proof of progress, which can yield much personal meaning and satisfaction.

Back to my example of writing this book. Because I have determined at the outset that this is important to me, I begin to set some goals that I think are realistic in terms of my time, abilities, and motivation. Just the process of thinking about specific goals seems to get me moving. When my goals and projected completion dates are written down on paper, that helps even more. At this moment I'm a little behind in meeting my goals—but they were somewhat unrealistic. Several tasks took slightly longer than expected, and I had some interpersonal concerns to sort out. There's no reason to panic; I simply readjust the goals to bring them in line with reality. At times I move ahead of my stated goals, usually when things seem to flow just right. On some days I may feel like I really need a break from writing. I take that break, but the next day I usually work twice as well—particularly if I know that my goal is to complete a certain amount by the end of the week.

I get a good feeling from fulfilling my goals. Self-directed achievement brings a feeling of self-control. It shows me that I can decide to do something that is important to me, and then do it. The achievement feels good, even if the goal is only a short-term one. Often this feeling is enough to keep me moving toward the next goal. I tell myself that I am pleased with myself . . . and I mean it! Sometimes, if the goal has been difficult to meet or if I'm tired or need a lift, I take a few days off, go to the mountains, spend time with family or friends, ski, canoe, see a movie, or just relax. I treat myself when I think I need or deserve a treat.

Once you decide that something is worth pursuing, you can apply goal setting and self-support in virtually any area of life. Whether you want to improve your focus control, win a championship, excel in business, run for your health, improve a relationship, or write a book, the basic procedure is the same. It is the focus of your commitment and the specific goals that are different.

Short-Term and Long-Term Goals

In sport your coach or a respected veteran athlete may be able to assist you in establishing realistic but challenging goals by helping you translate your overall aims into specific tricks, moves, plays, times, programs, routines, scores, or performance levels. A series of short-term goals that relate to your long-term goals should be established, with specific target dates for achievement. Achieving a goal, even a short-term one, makes you feel good and acts as a stimulus to pursue the next goal, thereby helping you to maintain motivation and build self-confidence.

Short-term goals might include mastering a certain skill, doing quality workouts, getting adequate rest, or completing a certain number of programs—today, by the end of the week, by the end of the month. Your short-term goals should help you improve not only physically but mentally; thus it's important to set goals for competition simulation, mental imagery, relaxation, positive thinking, and focus control.

Long-term goals may include the routine or program you'll need for a championship event; the speed, distance, time, or skills you want to attain by the end of this year and in the following year; or a good performance or a personal best in an important competition.

If you can write down your goals in concrete terms (I will be doing this by this time) you have a greater chance of accomplishing your objectives, and in less time than you otherwise would. How many practice days are left before your first game, your trials, your championship, your most important goal? Record your goals and the number of days remaining before important events to stimulate additional commitment in training.

Many top athletes keep daily training logs and competition diaries to direct and monitor their own progress. By listing goals set and met, recording training programs followed, and noting mental factors relating to best and less than best practices and competitions, you can enhance your progress and learn more from your experiences.

Think about tomorrow's goals tonight before you go to sleep or in the morning before you get out of bed. Just lie there for a few minutes and run through your mind what you want to accomplish today. This sets the stage for doing what you want to do every day.

It is important that you set your own goals, rather than having someone else set them for you. Your decision increases your commitment and motivation. Shared goal setting—for example, between you and your coach, you and your parents, or you and your partner—is valuable as long as you have personally weighed the situation and feel that the goal is what *you* really want.

For most people, selecting their own goals and having ample input into their training program is the most effective means for reaching their potential. I know that this is true for most high-performance athletes, and it's also true for me. I know better than anyone else what I have done and what I want to do. I also know better than others what will help me and what I need at a particular moment.

Input and feedback from others are also extremely important and can be very meaningful if they are constructive and well targeted. Still, you are a unique individual. No one else is exactly like you. If you are to be your best, you and those around you must respect your differences. It is often the differences that lead to greatness.

Setting and pursuing your personalized goals helps you to know yourself better, to extend yourself farther, and to offer what you are capable of offering to yourself and to others. If you really want to explore and expand your own potential, you must set individualized goals. They will likely become less formal as you become more experienced with the process, but they will still be there and continue to work for you.

Moving Toward Your Goals

Excellence in any field depends largely on three basic factors: (a) how well you know where you want to go, (b) how much you really want to get there, and (c) how strongly you believe in your ability to arrive at your desired destination.

Your performance is largely a function of your expectations for yourself. If you treat yourself as if you have something to offer, as if you have a contribution to make, as if you have a lot of potential, then you will behave accordingly. If you treat yourself as if you have little or nothing to offer, then this will likewise be reflected in your performance. Don't sell yourself short! You have a whole lot more to offer than most people recognize. How can I say that? I don't even know you, right? Well, if you are anything like other members of the human species whom I have encountered, you have all kinds of untapped potential. And if you pick up a book like this, you probably have visions of realizing some of that potential.

I once worked with a cross-country skier who was overflowing with natural talent. However, he didn't think he could be a great athlete because he had no "proof"; that was what he wanted in order to believe in himself. One way of providing this proof, which can boost your confidence in your real potential, is to chart your progress systematically so that you can see your improvement. Another way is to train or compete with some highly respected athletes so you realize that they are human too and that you can hang in there with them at least for certain parts of training or competition. Begin looking for what is good in yourself and in your performance instead of always looking for what is bad. Remind yourself of what you do well (for example: The approach is good, the follow-through is great.), and give yourself suggestions for improvement in a positive and constructive manner (for example: Good speed coming in; I could try to get my weight off that foot a little quicker; let's give it a try.). Walk out there and try being totally positive with yourself. You will have a better workout. You will feel better, and it might even rub off on those around you whom you care about.

We all start with one constant: There are 24 hours in a day! If I'm training or working toward a specific goal, I might as well dig in and do as much quality work as I can while I'm there. If I mentally prepare myself to complete every task as efficiently as I can, with the highest quality of effort, I can meet my goals and still have time for myself, my family, and my friends. By organizing your time—planning your workout and setting specific daily goals—you can accomplish more while you are working out and still leave time for adequate rest and the other joys in life. You can even schedule some relaxation time, some fun time, some free time.

Three students in my sport psychology class, to fulfill a behavior observation project, decided to observe some local gymnasts working out. What they recorded was the actual time each gymnast spent on the apparatus during a 2-hour workout. The average time was about 10 minutes. How much time do you spend actively involved in high-quality training in your specific event during a practice? Could you be using your time more effectively? Probably. But you have to be careful not to go overboard in the other direction. You can't be expending physical effort every second. You need time to think, to evaluate previous performances, to mentally prepare for a high-quality effort, to rest and reflect, to interact with other athletes, and sometimes to goof around.

I guess it all boils down to what you want at different stages, or within different components, of your life. If it doesn't really matter to you whether you use your time more efficiently or whether you improve much in a particular area—forget the performance charts and the striving for excellence, and focus on getting what you want out of the experience . . . fun, fitness, social interaction, the wind and sun on your face, or whatever you are seeking. There is absolutely nothing wrong with making that decision. But if you want to excel in a particular field, then a major commitment is required. Before making this kind of commitment you have to be quite sure that the goal, or the overall process of striving to reach it, is important enough to you to warrant your commitment. Often we know intuitively whether something is worth pursuing with commitment. Other times it is helpful to discuss our feelings with the people closest to us. It's also possible to raise some specific questions that will either increase your commitment or free you to pursue other endeavors. For example, if you decide to pursue a goal with commitment, ask yourself these questions:

- What do you expect to gain?
- What do you expect to lose?
- What will be the gains for other important people in your life?
- What will be the losses for these people?

- Do you think it's really worth the effort when there are no guarantees of outcome?
- Why do you want to do this?

If you think about each of these questions and respond to them honestly (perhaps in writing), the issue will be clearer in your own mind, and you should be in a better position to make a decision that is right for you. Once you recognize that you do have a choice, and you make a conscious decision in either direction, you can often approach things in a more positive light. If the decision is to "go for it" and you are dedicated to this choice, you will have a greater capacity to endure the demands that follow. It was Nietzsche who wrote that "he who has a reason why can bear with almost any how."

You can sometimes bolster your commitment by talking with family members, fellow athletes, coaches, or friends about your decision or your goals. Some athletes go so far as to make a public statement about their goals in an attempt to maintain or increase their motivation to pursue them. Most of us do not gain from making our goals public, but we can all gain from the support and encouragement of important people in our lives as we attempt to pursue our personal goals.

When goals set clash with goals met, it is helpful to remember that unmet goals, plateaus, times of seemingly little or no progress, even periods of backsliding are natural . . . and are experiences that everyone faces at some point. Progress is a series of ups and downs; it is by no means all clear sailing. Even when you see no obvious signs of improvement, you may still be laying the groundwork for future progress. Think of the best athlete in your sport: He has also been discouraged. She has also had problems to overcome and goals she has not met. But somehow that person persists and overcomes the obstacles. That is part of the *path to excellence*. It is also part of the path of day-to-day living.

It's no tragedy not to meet a particular goal. You grow from the experience, learn from it, adjust your goal, stick some short-term goals or intermediate steps in front of it. A temporary setback doesn't mean that you have to quit or give up on your goals. It means that you work on setting more short-term goals or more appropriate goals, and that you readjust goals as you come to know yourself and your present situation better. Your goal may simply be to do, or cope, the best you can on that day.

When I was actively competing in gymnastics, I used goal setting in a haphazard way. Now that I am more knowledgeable in this area, I am better able to set very specific goals and to adjust unmet goals by bringing them into line with me, rather than trying to force myself into line with them. When there is a discrepancy, the goals are usually off target.

I am being what I am. I am doing the best that I can at this moment, given the complexities of life. Goal setting doesn't provide all the answers, but when used properly it certainly does nudge you in the direction you want to go. Regardless of what you want to accomplish, goal setting and on-going self-support are important. To think more positively, focus more completely, or be more relaxed at a particular time, set some short-term goals to work on today, tomorrow, and every day. Put your goals up on the wall as a reminder. Give it a try. You've got nothing to lose and a lot to gain in terms of living closer to your potential.

Chapter 5

☐

Changing Perspectives

The one thing over which you have absolute control is your own thoughts.
It is *this* that puts you in a position to control your own destiny.
Paul G. Thomas

The key to living closer to your potential both in sport and outside of sport lies in developing your ability to keep matters in perspective and view things in a constructive way.

Whenever an important event is about to occur in your life, thoughts run through your head about the meaning and probable consequences of the event. You say certain things to yourself or believe certain things about what might happen and what it will mean. These thoughts make you feel anxious or free you from anxiety, make you feel confident or shatter your confidence.

What triggers your emotional reaction to an event is the way you perceive the event, or what you say to yourself about yourself in relation to it, rather than the event itself. A simple change in your perception about the meaning of a particular event, or in your belief about your capacity to cope with it positively, can change your current emotional reality. Nothing changes except the way you perceive yourself or interpret the event, and yet that change can give you inner strength and confidence, can free you from anxiety, fear, guilt, depression, or self put-down.

Let's take anxiety as an example. "You can almost hear the tension out there . . . this is it . . . do or die . . . the world is watching . . . there's *real* pressure on these athletes here today." If you listen to anxiety-casters and actually start to believe what they say, you might begin to believe that anxiety is external and inescapable, like rain pouring down from a dark cloud. Yet some athletes are able to enter these "anxious" situations and stay focused without becoming overly anxious themselves. They perform well under the cloud without being dampened by anxiety. How is that possible? It is possible for the simple reason that anxiety doesn't float around out there waiting to pounce on you like some kind of bogeyman.

It is strictly internal; in fact, anxiety does not exist outside your head. Certain situations may tend to make you anxious, but you are not *required* to become anxious in these situations. Situations are not anxious, people are. You are anxious when you accept the situation as one that creates anxiety, or when you become overly concerned with outcomes or consequences. Athletes who can enter the arena feeling "up" but in control have repainted the anxiety-filled picture that others have often painted for them.

People often wait until anxiety arises to seek strategies for coping with it. They do not focus enough attention on the ways to prevent unproductive anxiety from arising in the first place. Various techniques for on-site anxiety control, including shifts in focus and relaxation, can be effective, but sometimes they don't get to the root of the problem—which is a person's acceptance of a situation as stressful. Your first line of anxiety prevention and control lies in your way of viewing yourself and the world around you. Above all you must keep your own worth in perspective, regardless of whether or not you meet a particular goal.

Anxiety and Self-Defeating Beliefs

We experience anxiety in sporting situations, as well as in other aspects of life, largely because of self-defeating beliefs. Albert Ellis (1976, p. 25) states them as follows:

1. The belief that you must *always* have love and approval from *all* the people you find significant
2. The belief that you must *always* prove to be thoroughly competent, adequate, and achieving
3. The belief that emotional misery comes from external pressures and that you have little ability to control or change your feelings
4. The belief that, if something seems fearsome, you must preoccupy yourself with it and make yourself anxious about it
5. The belief that your past remains all-important and that, because something once strongly influenced your life, it has to keep determining your feelings and behavior today

The first two beliefs set you up for a lifetime of frustration because they are impossible goals. You cannot have the love and approval of all people at all times, no matter how much you give of yourself; nor can you always be thoroughly competent at all things. None of us are, or ever will be, perfect at all things at all times. We all screw up sometimes, and that's OK. That's being human.

The excessive anxiety that destroys skilled performance usually comes from exaggerating the importance of an event's outcome, from viewing it as if your physical or emotional life is at stake or as if your entire meaning on earth rests in the balance. We know this is not really the case, but we sometimes act as if it were. On rare occasions, in some high-risk sports, a physical life may hang in the balance. But never is our emotional life or overall meaning really on the line in a sport performance, no matter how much we may tell ourselves, or how much others may lead us to believe that it is.

If you approach a big competition as if it is the only important event in the world, as if your life will be completely useless unless you do well, then you set yourself up for needless and unproductive anxiety. If you incessantly worry about your performance or about appearing incompetent, you are probably too focused on negative possibilities or too concerned with what others might think. The worry is almost always worse than the event itself. Your performance (and people's reaction to it) rarely turns out to be as terrible as you might have imagined. But it would turn out a lot better if you did not dwell on the negative images in the first place. You can lessen your worries and improve your performance by viewing yourself, the event, and your performance in a more positive light.

The best athletes approach competitions physically activated and mentally (task) focused. "I've got a job to do, I'm capable of doing it, and I'll do it the best I can. Beyond that I'm not going to worry about it." If they do have a subpar performance they draw out the positive lessons and move on. They have learned to focus effectively and to keep things in perspective. Think about your own situation: At one time you were no good in your sport at all—in fact, you hadn't even begun to participate in it. Yet you were an acceptable person and loved by those closest to you. Now that you are so much more skilled, why is it so disastrous to achieve a little less than perfection? You are still a skilled athlete, a worthy human being, and you will continue to be acceptable and worthy after you stop competing.

I can no longer do a quadruple twisting back somersault on a trampoline; it's been over 10 years since I've done a triple; I can still do a double. Does that mean that I am half as good, half as worthy a person as I used to be? Does it mean that I'm twice as good a person as someone who cannot do even a single somersault? It would be ridiculous to think that my overall value as a person depends on my performance on any given night, but we sometimes do confuse the outcome of a performance with our human worth. When this happens, a more balanced perspective is needed: Our human essence extends far beyond our performance in a given task at a given time.

Setting Goals to Reduce Anxiety

The best way to permanently reduce unwanted and unproductive anxiety is to set realistic personal performance goals, to focus on doing the things that will help you meet the challenge successfully, and to know in your heart that you remain a valued person regardless of the performance outcome. If you can approach anxiety-provoking situations with a healthy perspective, then most debilitating anxiety will not surface. You will become positively energized, because you are excited and you need a certain level of activation to perform well in your event. But you will not become anxious or upset to a degree that will jeopardize your focus during performance or your well-being afterward.

How do you go about changing perspectives? You begin by questioning some of your own thoughts—the ones that upset you in the first place. The next time you feel upset, stop and ask yourself: Why am I upset? What am I thinking or saying to myself that is making me upset? Does the event, or my performance, or people's reaction really mean what I'm telling myself it means? Do I *have to* upset myself over this? Is it really worth continuing to upset myself about this? Is it doing me or anyone else any good?

Set a personal goal to think less in ways that are likely to upset you and more in ways that will help you. Look for the legitimate support within yourself and your environment that can give you the strength and balance to deal with the stresses in your life. Tell yourself new, positive things about yourself and your capacity to meet the challenges you face. You are fully capable of changing your perspective if you constantly remind yourself to think in more positive ways.

Some people find that *mental imagery* helps with this positive change process. Think about how you would prefer to respond in various situations. Imagine yourself responding more effectively to situations that may have upset you unnecessarily in the past. Imagine yourself in the situation, thinking, focusing, believing, and acting in more constructive and less anxious ways. Then work on replicating this vision of yourself in the real world. With persistence you'll win this one.

Sometimes just a conscious attempt to see things from a different perspective, or as they could be, leads to a change in the way you view a situation or yourself. As soon as you begin to tell yourself (and believe)— Hey, that doesn't really matter; There's no reason to get upset about this; This doesn't mean I'm inadequate; That's not what he really thinks at all— changes in your feelings are apparent. As soon as you begin to recognize and believe in your own worth and abilities—Hey, I can do this; I can direct my own thoughts and focus; I can control my reactions—there's nearly always an immediate change in your behavior.

Whenever you are able to influence a positive change in your focus or perspective, think about what you did or said to yourself to bring it about. Hang on to this for future use. Also try to be aware of self-imposed obstacles to positive change, such as things you say to yourself that block your own progress: I can't do this; I'm no good, stupid, or slow; I'll probably mess it up; and the likes. What are you saying to yourself right now about your capacity to change the things you want to change? That's a good place to start establishing a positive perspective.

Sometimes relabeling or reinterpreting your physical sensations is enough to put you back in control. Let's say that you get a knot in your stomach or your heart starts to thump hard just before a competition begins. You could say to yourself, Oh God, I'm so nervous . . . I don't know what I'm going to do. . . . I'll probably blow it. Or you could interpret these physical cues in a totally positive manner, and say, The knot in my stomach is the result of the secretion of adrenalin, which acts as a stimulant; what is actually happening is that my body is telling me I'm ready, let's go! Virtually every athlete you have ever seen or competed against, including all the best athletes in the world, experience this sensation before an important event. They make it work for them by recognizing its positive elements and by channeling their focus to their task.

A certain amount of activation is necessary for good performance in physical endeavors. You wouldn't do too well if you were half asleep. You are looking for that optimal amount of "upness" where you feel just right. If you find yourself feeling too pumped up, you can also make this work for you by using it as a signal to try to bring yourself down a bit, perhaps through relaxation or refocusing.

It is important to remember that, no matter how you viewed things in the past, you are not obligated to keep viewing them in the same light. You may have thought of yourself as being necessarily anxious or reactive in certain situations in the past, but you now recognize that you can control and change how you feel about the situation, as well as how you react in the situation. By working to maintain a positive perspective and talking to yourself in a constructive way, you can enter more situations in control, even situations that previously caused anxiety or performance problems.

Suppose that, at the competition site, your thoughts start to drift to such things as how good your competitors look, how unfair the officials might be, how nervous you are, how terrible it would be if you blew it. What can you do about it? Use these thoughts as a reminder to think more constructively; to remember your overall value as a person; to recall your simple goal of just doing the best you can do today; to relax; to focus your attention on your own preparation, your own warm-up, and doing your job—all of which are within your own control. Remind yourself of your best performance focus, your good recent workouts, and your capability to perform well. Self-assuring thoughts about your worth, your preparation, your readiness, your commitment, your capacity, and your best focus can help immensely, and they are based on facts—solid, positive facts.

Many important things, such as your performance, your health, and your perspective, are potentially within your control. Once you realize that you can effect change in these areas, you will, precisely because they are within your control. However, other important things in life are beyond your potential control. It is self-defeating to take responsibility or feel guilty for things that happen to you, or to others close to you, over which you have no direct influence. You cannot control things that are impossible to control no matter how hard you try or how much responsibility you assume for doing so. You cannot control the past; you cannot control things that occur strictly by chance; you cannot control the actions, reactions, or incompetencies of all the people around you.

Your energy and your goals are best served when you focus on things within your potential control. Your thoughts are within your control. Your thoughts direct your focus, beliefs, and performance. Think about failure and you become anxious. Think about errors and they are yours. Think about your strengths and you feel strong. Think that you *can*, and you *will*.

These positive self-suggestions can help you in your balanced pursuit of personal excellence:

- I am in control of my own thinking, my own focus, my own life.
- I am a good, valued person in my own right.
- I control my own thoughts and emotions, and direct the whole pattern of my performance, health, and life.
- I am fully capable of achieving the goals that I set for myself today. They are within my control.
- I learn from problems or setbacks, and through them I see room for improvement and opportunities for personal growth.
- My powerful mind and body are one. I free them to excel.
- Every day in some way I am better, wiser, more adaptable, more focused, more confident, more in control.
- I choose to excel.

Part II

Paths to Excellence

Preceding page: Larry Cain, silver medalist at 1000 meters, 1989 World Canoeing Championships.

Chapter 6

□

Self-Assessment and Strategy Selection

Change and growth take place when a person has risked himself and dares to become involved with experimenting with his own life.
H. Otto

The pursuit of excellence begins with getting to know your own patterns. This is simply a process of becoming more aware of your own capabilities, strengths, and weaknesses. It also means becoming more aware of what you really want, as opposed to what others want of you. With this awareness you can better establish priorities and thereby pursue the things that are really important to you and avoid the things that are not.

You know yourself better than anyone else in this world. You are already inside yourself. You just have to begin tuning in to how you usually think, feel, and react in different situations; how you relate to different types of people and events in your life; and how you cope with different kinds of demands. Sports settings provide beautiful opportunities for knowing yourself. You can listen to your body and associated feelings. You can discover your best focus for meeting various challenges. What do you tell yourself, think to yourself, or sense when your situation improves or degenerates? How do you turn it around? Take time to know yourself.

Getting to know your own sport-related patterns also involves becoming aware of the direction of your own errors. Do you usually err by overreacting or underreacting, by overrotating or underrotating? Do you usually spin too hard or not hard enough? Do you open up too early or too late? Do you usually miss when fresh or fatigued, to the left or right of the target, high or low? Do you overthrow or underthrow? Are you too activated or not activated enough? Are there any patterns to your competitive errors? Finding out what they are is a first step toward improvement.

Assessing Focus Control and Commitment

The following two self-assessment scales are based on qualities that lead-ing coaches and athletes around the world use to describe the kind of commitment and self-control that separates the good player from the great player in a variety of sports. A rating of 5 means that the statement is com-pletely true, a rating of 1 means that it is completely false, and a rating of 3 means that it is sometimes true and sometimes false.

Focus Control Rating Scale

Focus Control.   Rate yourself on each item. Then go back and look at your strengths as well as the areas in which you need to improve.

1. I can avoid becoming too nervous or too uptight at competitions.

   1   2   3   4   5

2. I get so absorbed in the performance (or experience) that everything else disappears.

   1   2   3   4   5

3. I can maintain or quickly regain a high level of focus control at practice.

   1   2   3   4   5

4. I can maintain or quickly regain a high level of focus control in competitions.

   1   2   3   4   5

5. I have inner confidence or a feeling of "I can do it."

   1   2   3   4   5

6. I take criticism well and learn from it.

   1   2   3   4   5

7. I can handle bad calls or decisions that go against me.

   1   2   3   4   5

8. I can stay motivated when behind or down in points.

   1   2   3   4   5

9. I can maintain focus totally in the present, living in the here and now (for example, one shot, one move, one stroke at a time).

   1   2   3   4   5

10. I can quickly regain my focus on the present performance even after an error.

$$1 \quad 2 \quad 3 \quad 4 \quad 5$$

Total Focus Control Score _____

Commitment Rating Scale

Commitment.   Rate yourself on each item. Then go back and look at your strengths as well as those items that may require reassessment or realignment if excellence is to become a realistic goal.

1. I am willing to sacrifice other things to excel in my sport (or other chosen endeavor).

$$1 \quad 2 \quad 3 \quad 4 \quad 5$$

2. I really want to become an outstanding performer in my sport (or other chosen endeavor).

$$1 \quad 2 \quad 3 \quad 4 \quad 5$$

3. I am determined to never let up or give up (for example, determined to get the point, make the move, or complete the run).

$$1 \quad 2 \quad 3 \quad 4 \quad 5$$

4. I take personal responsibility for mistakes and work hard to correct them.

$$1 \quad 2 \quad 3 \quad 4 \quad 5$$

5. I give 100 percent in practice (whether it's going well or not so well).

$$1 \quad 2 \quad 3 \quad 4 \quad 5$$

6. I give 100 percent effort in competitions or performances (whether down or up in points).

$$1 \quad 2 \quad 3 \quad 4 \quad 5$$

7. I put in extra time for mental and physical preparation before, after, or between regular practice sessions.

$$1 \quad 2 \quad 3 \quad 4 \quad 5$$

8. I push hard even if it hurts.

$$1 \quad 2 \quad 3 \quad 4 \quad 5$$

9. I feel more committed to improvement in my sport (or other chosen endeavor) than to anything else.

    1   2   3   4   5

10. I feel more enjoyment, fulfillment, or importance in my sport (or other chosen endeavor) than in anything else.

    1   2   3   4   5

Total Commitment Score _____

Athletes who excel rate themselves higher on both commitment and focus control than less accomplished athletes. They tend to have total scores of 40 or above on both the commitment scale and the focus control scale, or average scores of 4 for individual items on both scales. The higher your commitment and the greater your focus control, the more likely you are to achieve your highest level of excellence.

What can you do once you have assessed your focus control and commitment? To improve your focus control, draw upon the various strategies presented in this book. Review your level of commitment. Given your current skill level, is your commitment strong enough to take you to your personal goals? If not, perhaps you can intensify your commitment to bring it into line with your goals. The other option is to adjust or lower your performance goals so that they are more realistic in terms of your present situation and current level of commitment; otherwise you may experience continued frustration.

Steps to Self-Growth

When working with athletes and other clients on performance enhancement, I often pose some basic performance-related questions to which they respond. Together we discuss various options for self-growth, some of which they implement. Over the past 15 years I have discovered that, with some basic guidelines to follow, many people are capable of asking themselves these same questions and can successfully choose their own self-growth strategies. Following are six procedural steps designed to help you explore your options for self-growth:

1. Select an area of focus that you would like to improve, or a situation over which you would like to have greater personal control. Choose a target on which to set your sights for positive change.
2. Complete the self-directed interview provided (p. 45) to pinpoint the circumstances within this situation that are related to your best

performances or greatest control and to your worst performances or least control.

3. Reflect closely on what may already have worked for you, and review the self-growth options provided in this book. Select some strategies that you feel may help you improve your situation or strengthen your positive focus.

4. Experiment with one or more of these strategies, first in a non-threatening situation (for example, in a practice) and then in a more stressful situation (for example, in a competition).

5. Keep a log to record the strategies that are effective for you, and make a note of what you do that makes them work.

6. Where feasible, get together with friends or teammates who are also working on becoming mentally stronger or more fully focused, to discuss the effectiveness of various strategies and the best ways to implement them.

If you approach this self-growth process seriously, it will be a valuable learning experience. You can use the interview questions and self-growth options to bring about desired improvements both in and out of sport. Thousands of people, including many national team athletes, have gone through and gained from this self-growth process, so I am confident that it can work for you. The final choice for self-growth always rests in your own hands.

Self-Directed Interview

The purpose of this interview is to clarify desired areas of improvement and specific targets for personal growth. A target may be something you are doing that you would prefer not to do, or something you are not doing that you would prefer to do. The precise circumstances that surround your best and worst performances in a specific situation should be thought out in detail before you select a self-growth strategy. It is very important to understand what you are already doing that sometimes improves a situation or your performance within it. If you keep a training log or performance diary, refer to it for detailed comments on how your thinking may have affected your performance positively or negatively in the past. If you don't keep a log, start one now for future reference.

It has become clear to me through my work with athletes that specific events within the environment and within a person's own thinking lead to performance problems. At certain moments, focusing seems to become a problem. For an Olympic figure skater this happened at important competitions, "when I see the nine judges on the ice peering over me as I begin my figures and I start to think about being judged instead of focusing on tracing the figure." For a world champion water-skier it was, "when I approach the first buoy on my slalom run and I think, oh-oh, I'm probably going to blow this." For a national team basketball player it was "when the coach yells at me during the game and I start to worry about him instead of concentrating on playing ball."

It is important to assess precisely when the problem arises and to become aware of what you are thinking or what you are focused on at that moment. The following self-directed interview questions are designed to help you make this self-assessment and to help you find your best focus for positive change. These interview questions have been used as a guide to improve relationships, strengthen focus, and enhance performance in and out of sport, so they should be relevant to your situation.

Self-Directed Interview Questions

1. What is the area or focus that you want to improve?

2. What are you doing that you don't want to do, or failing to do that you would like to do?

3. Where, when, and under what circumstances does a problem usually come up? In what situations (at home, at school, in practice, within competitions)? When certain kinds of demands are placed on you? When you think in certain ways?

4. How important is it for you to improve or change this situation?

5. Think about the times when you have been in this situation and your focus, your response, or your performance has been at its best. What was going on then? What were you doing or saying to yourself? What were you focused on?

6. What about the times when your focus or your performance seemed at its worst? What was going on then? What were you doing or saying to yourself? Where was your focus?

7. What seems to be the major difference between your best and worst experiences or performances:
   a. In what you are thinking about before the experience or performance?
   b. In what you are focused on during the experience or performance?
   c. In what others around you are doing or not doing?

8. What do you think you can do to improve the situation?

9. Have you made a strong enough commitment to regularly *practice* improving your focus control in this area? Are you prepared to make that commitment now?

Selecting a Self-Growth Strategy

Once you have completed your self-directed interview, you are faced with the task of selecting an effective self-growth strategy. "How do I choose one?" you're asking, right?

In chapters 7 to 14, I present those self-growth strategies that I use most often in my individual consultation with athletes and others pursuing personal excellence. Other strategies exist, but none have worked better than those I have outlined here.

Before choosing a strategy for a particular area of improvement, read through the various options, along with the case studies that show how people have used them. Keep in mind where you want to end up. Some approaches will be immediately more attractive to you than others, or will simply seem more suitable for you and your situation. You may read about a strategy and think, That will never work for me . . . and you will probably be right. As you read about another strategy, you might find yourself thinking, Hmm, maybe that one will work. You should try any strategy that makes intuitive sense to you. If it feels right just reading about it, try it.

Through my consultation with thousands of athletes, one thing has come through loud and clear—the uniqueness of mental preparation, motivation, and coping. An approach that may work beautifully for you may have the totally opposite effect on someone else. For example, in the same precompetition situation, one athlete can best prepare by thinking about something pleasant away from sport, another prefers to focus on the task at hand, and a third actually tries to focus on the anxiety and its sensations. Each approach works, but does so for uniquely different individuals.

Your belief about the potential effectiveness of a particular strategy influences your commitment to work on it and, consequently, how well it will work for you. Usually your beliefs about what might be effective for you do not grow out of a vacuum; they are the result of many years of living with yourself. It would be difficult to have lived this long without knowing something about how you function. So your beliefs about what will or will not work for you often rest on a sound foundation. They are based on the number of years you have lived and the extent to which you have experimented with your own life. Try to read through the options with an open mind. Then follow your gut feelings on strategy selection.

It is best to select several strategies that seem appropriate for your particular situation. Then experiment with these strategies until you can isolate what works best for you. It may be a single approach, a combination of several interrelated approaches, or a personal strategy that you have come up with yourself. Often all that you need is more persistence in practicing and implementing the strategies that have already been somewhat successful in your past. If something works for you, then use it, because that's the bottom line.

Chapter 7

□

Gaining Control

Control your emotion or it will control you.

Athletes who consistently perform close to potential have learned to control their focus, channel their emotions, and bounce back from setbacks in a constructive way. They have refined the ability to shift quickly from negative thinking to a positive focus, particularly in response to increased anxiety, errors, or setbacks. If you don't learn to do this, your chances of getting the most out of your training sessions and the best out of yourself when it counts most will be dramatically reduced. The mental skills required for high levels of excellence are developed long before the day of the contest through countless hours of practice, and through experiences that teach you to maintain or regain control over your own mental state.

Reacting to Errors

Constructive reaction to errors or setbacks is a learned process. Many people react to the loss of points or games by becoming upset with themselves, angry at others, or depressed. If they fall behind they may lose control, cease to perform well, or feel like giving up. The earlier you learn to react in a positive or constructive way, the better.

A setback within a game (for example, loss of ball, serve, point, or game) can serve as a reminder to focus more fully on critical performance cues, to redirect your energy in a positive way, or to analyze losses at an appropriate time. After games the best players often mentally replay key moves and turning points, discuss the game with their teammates or coaches, and always try to find lessons that will help them for future games. They may experience disappointment, anger, or frustration, but they learn to pass through it quickly by extracting constructive lessons that can help them in the future. As one of the world's best badminton players expressed it, "As a less experienced player I reacted more emotionally, I was angry at myself. Now I concentrate more, analyze errors or losses, replay key shots and turning points, and draw out important lessons."

One player experienced real problems with emotional outbursts during games. "If I lost a rally, I hated my opponent. . . . I would get so angry that I could lose 8 points in a row because of that. I had problems controlling my temper to the point of shouting and breaking rackets." He made a strong effort to get his temper and focus under control. When he played with controlled focus he played as well as anyone. One strategy he used when he got angry was to try to take advantage of his anger by constructively directing his aggressive energy in the next rally to "hustle more," "be more ready," "move faster," and "smash harder." This shifted his focus away from himself or his opponent and got him back into playing the game with a renewed vigor.

What's wrong with getting angry or upset after making an error? Most of all it interferes with your reason for being there, whether you are seeking enjoyment or an ultimate performance. Its effects are probably most detrimental if you begin to condemn yourself during the program, event, or game, because you take your focus away from the remaining tasks. If you are mentally chastising yourself because of the last shot, move, or event, you cannot at the same time be focusing on the present skill or preparing for your next move. You can't dwell on how you blew the last routine and at the same time perform well in this routine. You have to clear your head from worries about what has passed to free your body and mind to perform in the present.

Someone who flies off the handle might say, Oh, but it doesn't matter that much if I do it during practices. Ah, but it does. If you become practiced at upsetting yourself for missed moves or poor events during training sessions, there's a very good chance it will carry over into competition. Moreover, it takes away the joy of sport. There are enough obstacles along the path to excellence; there is no advantage in adding self-put-downs. Staying positive, relaxed, and focused is particularly important for regaining the flow of a performance after an error during a game, a break in a routine or program, or an attempt that fails. It is essential for coming back from behind. If you do not learn to pass quickly from negative thoughts to a constructive performance focus, the game will rapidly slip away from you.

To speed up your learning process, think about how you can best respond to setbacks, establish personal goals for improving your focus control, and work toward achieving those goals. The next time something goes wrong in a game or a routine, use that as a signal to focus on what you know will enhance the rest of your performance. For example, during a gymnastics routine, a skating program, or team game, let any thoughts about the error slip away by concentrating fully on the next move or perhaps on a flash of finishing well. In a sport where there is a break from intense concentration, such as a racket sport, it is possible to quickly analyze the reasons for the error (for example, while walking back to receive the serve); take a deep, relaxing breath; and focus on an appropriate performance reminder for the next point.

You may have excellent physical and technical skills, but you will never perform to your full capacity unless you gain control of your mental state. You must be in control mentally; you must be mentally strong.

This was a lesson learned through experience by a top Swedish sportsman. As a rookie he quickly discovered that, as soon as he got upset, he couldn't play well. He grew, as a result of this knowledge, into a veteran with a different approach: "I practiced reacting the way I wanted to react, which changed my feeling going into the game. I could go in with more confidence. . . . I tried to think about what caused a mistake and correct it. I thought about what made me lose and analyzed it. I was disappointed, but I tried to learn from it." This man's early recognition of the critical importance of focus control, along with his conscientious attempt to continually improve, allowed him to become one of the best in the world.

Cases in Self-Control

Pat Messner, former world champion in waterskiing, reflected on how she went about gaining greater personal control in practice and in competition.

> I first began competition when I was 10 years old. At that time, I felt that having days where nothing goes right and everything goes wrong, days where I felt I was the worst competitor on earth, and days when I would be mad at anything, was all part of the competitive life.
>
> I was wrong, and it wasn't an easy thing to find out. It happened because of an experience I had in the Western Hemisphere Championship in Mexico. It was in March and that was during our off-season. During the practice session I couldn't do anything right. I had never skied as badly. This practice session made me believe that there was no way I was going to place . . . let alone win! I decided I might as well relax and enjoy myself.
>
> Before the actual event I went through my usual stretching and warmup. The only difference was that I wasn't thinking about what was to come. I just sat down on the grass, listened to some music, and

waited for my turn. This was very unusual for me because I'm usually very nervous. I just didn't seem to care. I listened to the music and relaxed.

Believe it or not, I've never had a better tournament. I skied better than I ever had before. Not only that, but I became Western Hemisphere Champion.

What did all this prove? It proved to me that if I could stay relaxed and calm at all my tournaments maybe I'd always ski better.

Since that time I have learned many things that may be as helpful to you as they were to me. I've tried a number of different methods of relaxation. The method I found best is a simple thing anyone can do anytime, anyplace. Sit down or lie down and listen to some relaxing music. I can take my portable cassette right down to the dock and listen to music till it's time for me to ski. I let my mind do what it likes. I don't take responsibility for my thoughts. I just let them pass by. If you don't like music, then try reading a book. I also found this to be very helpful.

Another important thing for me is mental practice. I run through my event mentally just as if it was real. I try to feel as if I am actually doing the run. If you find it hard to "feel" yourself or you can't picture yourself, get someone to take a film of you. Sometimes it helps to give yourself audio cues as you go. I also try to simulate as many tournament conditions as possible so that if unusual conditions should occur, I won't be as affected by them.

Sometimes it seems that the better you are, the easier it is to get upset by "little" things. I found that if I moved my attention away from what was making me angry and thought about something else, I'd feel better. Sometimes I set a goal for myself, like, The next two out of three times I get a chance to get mad, I won't. Most days it worked pretty well. On other days, the more I tried not to get mad or upset, the madder I got. It's days like that when I'm probably better off having a day of rest rather than practicing. Continuing to practice when I'm upset accomplishes absolutely nothing.

To try to improve her focus control during practices, Pat did a self-growth project following the procedures outlined in this book. Her goal was to make the best of as many practice sessions as possible in preparation for the world championships. Here are three self-control strategies she chose:

- *Relax.* Try to physically relax yourself . . . calm yourself. Take deep breaths and feel your body get loose as you exhale. Relax and try easier, just like when you won the Northern Hemisphere Championship. Pat and her coach tried a little experiment. "Each time I frowned he'd tell me, and I'd try to correct the situation. I found that when I did, my whole body felt more relaxed and I could do the trick easier."

- *Focus on correction.* Focus your attention on how to correct mistakes, instead of thinking about not having done something as well as you could and getting mad at yourself. If there are any errors, repeat the move mentally, correcting the errors, before trying it again. When practice is going well, write down what you think might be some of the reasons for it. Refer to this list to improve future situations.
- *Encourage yourself.* Avoid statements such as, You dummy; You can't do anything right; You will never make it to the World Tournament; Give up. Remind yourself of the facts. You are Canadian Champion and among the best in the world. It's not that you can't do anything right, you're simply doing one little thing wrong. Praise yourself for all the things you are doing right. You have a lot to be proud of; encourage yourself.

Pat experimented with each of the above strategies, sometimes stopping practice for 5 minutes to attempt to change her mood. As she said, "If you do not change the way you feel, the rest of the practice will be a waste of time." She found all of these strategies effective but none of them perfect. They worked well most of the time, but every now and then, no matter what she tried, she still got upset. Under these circumstances, Pat sometimes found it helpful for her coach to remind her of what she had accomplished, or to point out that she was being silly. "My behavior either got corrected, or he convinced me to take the day off." She found it most helpful to have a coach "who makes me realize that I'm only human."

If, after multiple attempts, a problem was not rectified, Pat could still leave practice knowing, You have given it a good shot, but it's not working today. Even though the problem is happening less and less, it still happens now and then. Everyone occasionally has a bad day or even a bad week. There's no sense getting upset about it. You are obviously much better than you are displaying at the moment. Why get upset? It won't do any good. Take the rest of the day off. Learn from it. Come in fresh tomorrow.

I can think of one incredibly gifted young athlete who could have gained from some of Pat's strategies for mood control. At age 11 she had Olympic potential. She could learn in two attempts what others often take 4 or 5 months to learn. But if she missed something or made an error, she cried, pouted, and stormed around for the rest of the day. According to her coach,

> If she makes an error in one of her routines during practice or during a competition, it throws her whole concentration off. She then gives up and either refuses to finish the routine or, if she does finish, it is done very poorly. If practice is not going well for her, she will cry, and the rest of the practice is ruined.

This young woman had visions of becoming an Olympic champion but instead retired after an unhappy 2 years because of an inability to get her moods under control. Perhaps if she had followed some of the strategies outlined here, her path would have unfolded in a different direction.

Sandy, a talented young female gymnast, had just made the team to compete in Europe. Since then she had had 2 weeks of consistently bad workouts. She and the coach had been arguing regularly, and her coach had not spoken to her at all for the last couple of days. She had 2 weeks left before departing for her first international competition.

The coach called to ask if I could help. Sandy and I stretched ourselves out on a blue mat in the corner of the gym and had a nice talk. She confirmed the bad workouts and arguments, and expressed a sincere concern about being ready for her meet in Europe. She told me that workouts usually started out OK but that she became moody when the coach said something negative, such as That's terrible; You don't listen; You don't try. At that point the workout would begin to slide. This led to more negative comments or no interaction, bad feelings, and some tears: overall, a lousy workout.

"Sandy," I said, "we know the coach isn't perfect, but then not many of us are. She says some very negative things, and I've talked to her about giving more positive comments. She's improving, but it's a difficult thing for her to do. An important point for you to keep in mind is that this is her way of trying to help you. She does care, and she does want you to improve—to be ready for the meet—and you want that too. At this point I think it is easier for you to control your reaction to her than it is to rely on her to change. You can, in fact, control your own moods if you really want to."

Sandy said she really did want to improve the gloomy practice mood and agreed to give the self-control approach a try.

"What do you feel when a bad mood begins?" I asked. "Are there physical sensations you are aware of? Are there certain emotions that begin to surface? Do you know when it's starting to happen?"

Sandy did have personal signals of an impending mood change, though she had never thought about them before. She discussed some of them, and I gave her this advice: "OK. When you start to experience these feelings—these personal signals—take a deep breath. Say to yourself, Relax. Then say to yourself, Turn this thing around . . . you want to have a good workout . . . she's here to help . . . you are not going to waste the night feeling lousy . . . you can control this. Then immediately focus on the trick you're trying to do or the routine you're trying to improve. Run it through your mind. Then go. *Do it.*

"Your challenge for the next week is to look for any signals of a bad mood coming on, and to turn it around before it gets to the destructive stage. Don't let it ruin your workout, and don't let it drive you to tears. You may not be successful in turning around every bad mood right away, but if you can do it even half the time, that's a big improvement. That's success. Even doing it once is better than what is happening now. Your ultimate goal is to be able to turn potentially bad situations into good ones all the time. You have the capacity to do this, and you are the only one who can do it because you are the person who controls your own thoughts and your own focus."

We devised a little mood chart to help Sandy assess her feelings and record her progress through the next 2 weeks (see pp. 56-60). At the start of each practice she recorded her prepractice mood on the Daily Mood Chart. For each event, she also recorded her mood at the start of the event, mood changes within the event, and her mood at the end of the event. If her mood had changed within the event she indicated this by marking the face to which it had changed. If it had changed more than once during the event, she drew an arrow from one face to the next, indicating the changes that took place. At the end of practice Sandy recorded her post-practice mood.

You can adapt this chart to suit your own needs. The comments section on the chart is primarily to help you discover what influences your mood. If your mood begins to decline and you are able to stop the slide or improve your disposition, then jot down what you did or said to yourself to turn things around. This will help you to discover what works best for you, as well as what does not work. You will then be in a better position to plug in things that work (for example, key words, images, or thoughts), whenever you need them.

Let's take a look at what happened to Sandy's mood control the first week:

Day 1. We discussed Sandy's concerns and the use of the mood chart approach.

Day 2. She started practice feeling happy and ended feeling so-so. Her pattern the previous week had been to start feeling happy and end feeling sad.

Day 3. She started practice feeling so-so and ended feeling very happy. She demonstrated to herself that she could lift her mood.

Day 4. She started practice feeling sad, actually feeling sick. She was

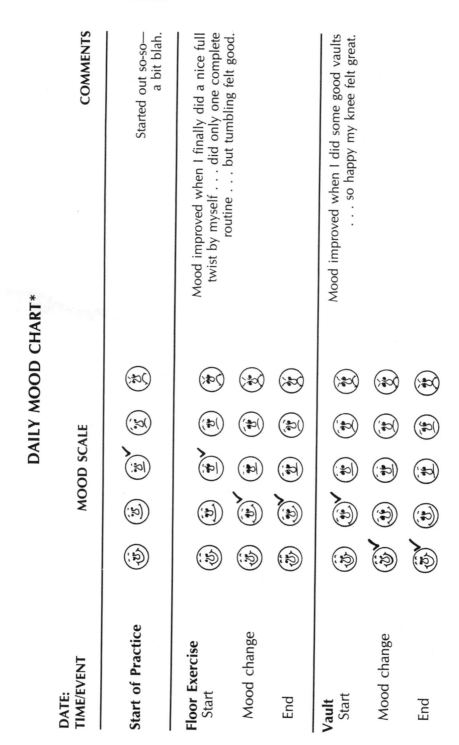

DAILY MOOD CHART*

DATE:

TIME/EVENT	MOOD SCALE	COMMENTS
Start of Practice		Started out so-so—a bit blah.
Floor Exercise Start		Mood improved when I finally did a nice full twist by myself . . . did only one complete routine . . . but tumbling felt good.
Mood change		
End		
Vault Start		Mood improved when I did some good vaults . . . so happy my knee felt great.
Mood change		
End		

Beam
Start

Mood declined when coach made a few criticisms. Beam wasn't too bad . . . did routines but not great.

Mood change

End

Bars
Start

Started out kinda bad, then coach yelled at me. Mood really declined. Said to myself "Stop"—"calm," finish strong. Then did a nice shoot handstand . . . and did about six routines. Felt really happy.

Mood change

End

End of Practice

Really happy—not 'cause overall workout was super . . . but I turned it around.

*This is a sample of a completed mood chart for one practice session in the sport of gymnastics. If you want a simplified recording of mood control progress, use the weekly chart.

WEEKLY PROGRESS CHART
MOODS

	Beginning Mood	Ending Mood	Strategy Most Successful	Comments
WEEK 1:				
Day 1	😣	😠		
2				
3				
4				
5				

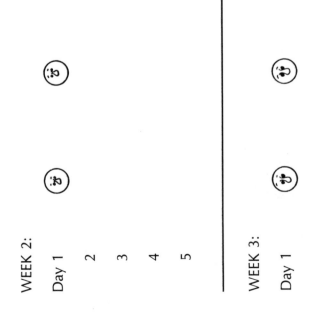

WEEK 2:

Day 1

2

3

4

5

WEEK 3:

Day 1

2

3

4

5

(Cont.)

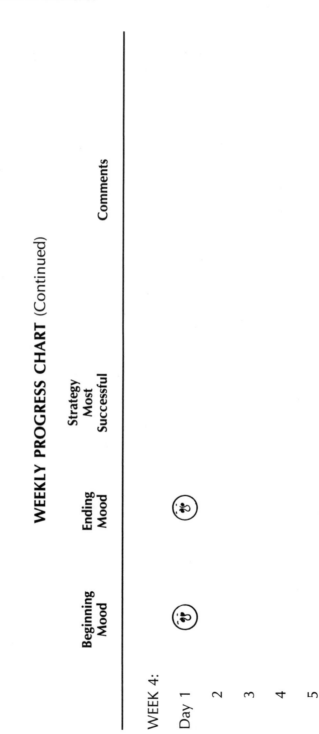

WEEKLY PROGRESS CHART (Continued)

	Beginning Mood	Ending Mood	Strategy Most Successful	Comments
WEEK 4:				
Day 1	🙂	🙂		
2				
3				
4				
5				

able to work through her low and end feeling happy after a productive workout.

Day 5. She started feeling happy and ended feeling very happy. She was starting to get things under control.

At the week's end Sandy and I went over her mood charts. Both of us were pleased with her progress. I asked her to think about a few things:

- What are your main signs of a bad mood about to come on?
- What has worked best for preventing or overcoming bad moods?
- What hasn't worked at all?
- Where can you focus for further improvement in mood control during the coming week?

Sandy's mood charts showed further improvement the following week, and she left for Europe feeling excited and more in control. As her self-awareness and her strategies for mood control continued to improve, the necessity for conscious attempts to control and chart her moods declined. She learned to maintain control more of the time and to solve many problems before they arose. If her mood did occasionally start to slide, she knew from experience that she could control it (almost all of the time).

Karin, a mediocre teenage gymnast, was very inconsistent in both practice and meets. One day she could hit everything well, and the next day she could blow everything. Karin told me that she knew whether it would be a good day or bad day before she got into the gym. If she had had a long day or felt at all sluggish, she would take that mood into the workout with her.

"Karin," I began, "unless you are seriously overtrained or ill, no matter how you feel on the way into the gym, you can turn things around to have a productive workout. Haven't you ever felt sluggish before practice and still had a good workout?" She had. "How is that possible? It is possible because you have the same body and the same skills that you had yesterday, when you had a good day. On your sluggish day, if your life depended on it, you could not only mount the beam, but you could jump over it and still have enough reserve energy to throw it across the gym.

"The next time you 'know you're going to have a bad day,' surprise yourself. Leave your negative thoughts in your locker. When you step through the gym door, energize! When you see that apparatus, challenge yourself to feel strong, feel energetic, feel radiant. Remind yourself why you are here. If you are here you might as well make the best of it. Why waste 3 hours? Try to focus fully for at least one event. Allow yourself to leave having had a good workout on something. If you can do it once, even in one event, you know you can do it again. When you do energize yourself on a sluggish day, try to be aware of how you have done it so you can do it again and again. You may not always have a super work-out, but most days can be good days, and you can make those not-so-good days better than they might otherwise have been."

Karin's pattern of being "up today, down tomorrow" was not restricted to training sessions. In her last competition she fell on every routine, even though she had done these same routines in practice. Why? "I knew I would have a bad day because I had a bad warm-up."

Does a warm-up that feels good or bad really have anything to do with your capacity to perform your routines in competition? Isn't a physical warm-up primarily to prepare your body for action, through stretching and movement? Haven't you ever seen someone have a lousy warm-up (for example, miss some tricks) and a great competition? It happens lots of times, and it can happen to you.

Your capabilities extend far beyond your warm-up. If you need a little proof, wait for a day when you come in feeling less than great in warm-up, and challenge yourself to a good performance. If you can do that once, in practice, you can go into the competition knowing and believing that even after a bad warm-up, things don't have to fall apart. You can still do your routines well. Figure skater Katarina Witt missed some important moves in her on-ice warm-up at the 1988 Olympic Games. She still nailed them in her routine and won the gold medal.

In the same way that your warm-up is separate from your performance on the first event, the first event is separate from the second event and the second from the third. A poor showing in one event, or on one skill, in no way means you must have a poor showing in the next. The thoughts that you have after blowing one thing are what set you up for blowing the next. If you are convinced that because you blew the last one, you will probably blow this one, then you probably will. Your body will shrug its shoulders and say, Who am I to argue with the thoughts and messages you are transmitting to me? If you, who are the master, say I'm going to blow it—I guess I'll follow orders and blow it.

On the other hand, if you know, as I know, that the next event or move really has nothing to do with the last one—that if you focus properly you are fully capable of performing at least as well as you ever have, regard-less of what you did the last time—then you free your body to explore its present potential.

If you think about your real capabilities, perhaps something will click and you will say to yourself, Hey, that's right—why should that affect this . . . it doesn't really have to. That may seem like a small step, but its im-pact can be gigantic. You may catch yourself thinking negatively from time to time (for example, You messed that up, so you'll probably mess this up too.). But if you have already thought about how ridiculous and unproductive that kind of thinking is and have preplanned something constructive to focus on, you can sometimes turn things around right on the spot. For example, you might say to yourself, Stop . . . that's ridiculous—this is a separate event—I can do as well here as I've ever done . . . now get focused and do it. You could also take a different tack: You've already blown one event, so what do you have to lose? Relax and enjoy it.

Let your thoughts encourage you and remind you of what you can do, then focus fully on doing it.

Mood Control

It's your mood! You can turn it around by thinking positive, happy, focused thoughts, almost anytime . . . or anywhere, in the morning, on the way to practice, or stepping onto the gym floor.

I can remember waking up one dull rainy morning, looking out the window, and thinking, Yuck, what a miserable day. But instead, I said to my mate, "Let's go out and enjoy the rain. Let's try to see the beauty of today in as many ways as possible." We turned that gloomy day around by laughing and smiling and enjoying the rain. What would otherwise have been a gray, drab day became one of beautiful gentleness and joy.

When you step out into the morning air, look for the good within the day and within yourself. Most mornings are beautiful, and there is beauty in every day—the sky, the dawn, the trees, the flowers, the sun, even the rain. Find the positive—It's a great day for a run; It's a super day for a game; It's a great day to be alive.

Mood control also means not upsetting yourself needlessly over little things or unfamiliar circumstances. It's important in sport and out of sport. When our athletes compete in Eastern bloc countries it is clear that the best performers are those who do not allow the food, the accommodations, or the system to negatively affect their performance mood. They view these things as relatively unimportant (which they are) and rely on the thoroughness of their overall mental and physical preparation. As one lad put it, "I'm one tough, finely tuned athlete." He proceeded to upset one of the top-seeded Soviet wrestlers in Moscow.

Thinking the right way when you get out of bed in the morning, particularly on an important day, can start you out on the right track. Try focusing on thoughts like these—Today is going to be a great day; I'm going to accomplish what I set out to do; I feel strong—I'm loaded with energy; I'm going to really live and experience this day.

Positive thinking can help put you in the right frame of mind, no matter how you are feeling when you first open your eyes to the dayligh. Make yourself feel the way you want to feel—productive and positiv

Mood control is an element of mind control, and it is within your grasp. It is largely a matter of looking for the good—in yourself, in your situation, in the world—and seeking out the gentleness of the storm.

Chapter 8

□

Mental Imagery

Your images lead your reality.

I'm sure mental images have run through your mind at some time or other. Let's see:

> Take a moment to think of your sport, a special person, your room, your favorite fruit, or a memorable experience. Do this now!

Did an image flash through your mind as you thought of any of these? You may not have called it mental imagery in the past, and perhaps you have not made use of your images in a highly refined or systematic way, but you have experienced it.

Before making an important phone call or while expecting a call, did you ever mentally rehearse what you would say? Through mental imagery you can prepare yourself to respond more effectively to expected—and unexpected—things that might happen.

Mental imagery gives you a chance to deal effectively with a problem or event in your head before you confront it in real life. If a problem does arise, you are better able to handle it or cope with it. This is largely because you have already faced the problem, have practiced some means of coping with it, and have overcome it in your mental reality, if not your physical reality. By using mental imagery, you can enter a variety of situations, including competitions, with feelings like I've been here before; It's no big surprise; There's no reason to panic; I can handle it.

Mental imagery can also be used to improve communication in social situations. Suppose that a young man calls a young woman unexpectedly and asks her to join him for dinner. She may grope hesitantly for a response—perhaps consenting when she really does not want to go, or refusing when she really would like to say yes. She could avoid this awkward situation by rehearsing a preferred approach or response for an unexpected call. Then, when a call does come, instead of stumbling around she can respond in a way that is in line with her true wishes. What's more, she will feel more comfortable, more relaxed, more in control.

I've used this approach in preparing to deal more effectively with unexpected requests for talks or workshops. There are a limited number of hours in your day and in your life. If you want to achieve certain goals, you must have priorities. So if I receive a request to do something that means taking time from another activity, I listen to the request politely, note the information, and say that I will check my schedule. After I'm off the phone, when I am alone and not pressured, I think about what the request entails in terms of my time, my priorities, and my various commitments. Do I really want to do this? Do I really have to do this? I often let such a decision work itself through while I'm running. Images of what the request entails often pop into my head. If at the end of my run I'm really excited about doing it, I agree; if not, I will most likely decline unless I feel a great obligation to say yes. Taking a bit of time to decide whether I want to do something puts me more in control of my life and, in this case, also lets me prepare to communicate my decision firmly, politely, and without feeling guilty. When I do say no, I always try to recommend someone else who can do a good job, who might appreciate the exposure and enjoy fulfilling the request.

Mental Imagery in Sport

In sport, mental imagery is used primarily to help you get the best out of yourself in training and in competition. The developing athletes who make the fastest progress and those who ultimately become their best make extensive use of mental imagery. They use it daily as a means of directing what will happen in training, and as a way of preexperiencing their best competition performances. Mental imagery often starts out simply, as you think through your goals, your moves, and your desired competitive performances. With practice it will develop to the point where, through imagery, you can draw on all of your senses to preexperience the achievement of many of your goals, moves, competitive performances, and coping strategies.

For many years an Olympic figure skater had experienced difficulties with a compulsory figure, the loop. I asked her to try to visualize herself doing the loop while she was sitting in a chair in my office. She was unable to imagine herself completing the loop. Either she would see herself making an error (the same one she usually made in the real world) and stop at that point, or the image would break up. I asked her to mentally practice doing the loop for approximately 10 minutes, every night for a week. We took it in steps: First she tried to get past the breaking point without worrying about her form—just get through it.

It took several nights of mental practice for her just to get by the breaking point in imagery. Once she got past this point, she began working on consistently getting through the complete figure in imagery without breaking. Finally, she focused on feeling herself do the loop as perfectly and fluidly as possible several times in a row. As soon as she began to feel herself skating the loop correctly in imagery, she also started to do it correctly in real-world practice situations. Within 2 weeks of our initial session, she was doing the best loops that she had ever done.

The skater usually did her mental imagery in the evening just before going to sleep. She would lie in bed, close her eyes, and try to call up the desired feeling as clearly as possible. Later she began to run through the figure in imagery just before actually doing it on the ice. Finally, while standing before the judges in a competition, she was able to look at the ice, map out her figure, and feel herself going through it; this set the stage for a good performance.

Many athletes find it helpful to imagine and feel themselves performing perfectly immediately before competitive performances. High jumpers feel their ideal jumps, divers their perfect dives, skiers their best runs, gymnasts their perfect routines; archers follow their arrows to the center of the target. Team sport athletes run through key offensive moves, quick transitions, and tough defensive moves. This process calls up the feeling of a best performance and focuses full attention on the task at hand. It serves as a last-minute reminder of the focus or feeling you need to follow in the game. It takes your mind off thoughts of worry or self-doubt, gives a boost to your confidence, and frees your body to perform. Doing mental imagery after a very successful performance, when the feeling is still fresh, can also be very valuable. It allows you to re-experience and hang on to successful aspects of the performance, which leads to further positive imagery and better performance. Some athletes find it especially helpful to increase their use of mental imagery when they have limited practice time (for example, at international events) or when recovering from an injury.

The Best Images

The world's best athletes have extremely well-developed imagery skills. They use imagery daily to prepare themselves to get what they want out of training, to perfect skills within training sessions, to make technical corrections, to imagine themselves succeeding in competition, and to strengthen their belief in their capacity to achieve their ultimate goal.

The refined performance imagery that highly successful athletes have developed almost always involves an inside view, as if they are actually doing the skill and feeling the action. Even the best athletes, though, did not initially have good control over their mental imagery. They perfected this mental skill through persistent daily practice.

Sylvie Bernier, a former Olympic champion in springboard diving, developed incredible imagery skills in preparation for her flawless Olympic performance in 1984.

> I did my dives in my head all the time. At night, before going to sleep, I always did my dives. Ten dives. I started with a front dive, the first one that I had to do at the Olympics, and I did everything as if I was actually there. I saw myself in the pool at the Olympics doing my dives. If the dive was wrong, I went back and started over again. It takes a good hour to do perfect imagery of all my dives, but for me it was better than a workout. I felt like I was on the board. Sometimes I would take the weekend off and do imagery five times a day. It took me a long time to control my images and perfect my imagery, maybe a year, doing it every day. At first I couldn't see myself, I always saw everyone else, or I would see my dives wrong all the time. I would get an image of hurting myself, or tripping on the board, or I would "see" something done really bad. As I continued to work at it, I got to the point where I could feel myself doing a perfect dive and hear the crowd yelling at the Olympics. But it took me a long time. I read everything about what I had to do, and I knew my dive by heart. Then I started to feel myself on the board doing my perfect dive. I worked at it so much, it got to the point that I could do all my dives easily. Sometimes I would even be in the middle of a conversation with someone and I would think of one of my dives and "do it" (in my mind).

Brian Orser, 1987 world champion in men's figure skating, reflected upon the "feeling" aspect of quality imagery.

> My imagery is more just feel. I don't think it is visual at all. I get this internal feeling. When I'm actually doing the skill on the ice, I get the same feeling inside. It is a very internal feeling that is hard to explain. You have to experience it, and once you do, then you know what you are going after. I can even get a feeling for an entire program. Sometimes in a practice I get myself psyched into a program that will win, like I won the long program last year. I step on the ice and go to my starting position and I get this feeling, "I'm at the Olympic Games," and I sort of get the whole program flashed before my eyes and I get this internal feeling how this program will be, and usually I'm fresh and usually it will be a perfect program. I don't just step out there in training and just say, Here we go, another program.

Lori Fung, former Olympic champion in rhythmic gymnastics, talked about using imagery for skill correction.

Sometimes I would think, Why did I miss that one move? Okay, I know what happened, I pulled my body in too close to the apparatus. Okay, now how do I avoid that? Then I try to see myself doing it correctly in imagery. I can actually see the apparatus coming down; I can see the stripe on the club as it rotates, the same way you'd see it when you're doing the routine; that's the best way. Most of the time I look at it from within, because that's the way it's going to be in competition. It is natural because I do the routines so many times that it's drilled into my head, what I see and how I do it. So if I think about a certain part of my club routine, or my ribbon routine, I think of it as the way I've done it so many times, and that's from within my body.

Kelly Kryczka, former world champion in synchronized swimming duet, discussed the use of on-site imagery.

We did a lot of imagery during training sessions, especially as the competition approached. When we were doing compulsory figures in practice, a minute before doing certain ones the coach would say, "Okay, you are going to do a 'best one.' You are going to do a whole compulsory figure." So before we went out there and did it, we would sit on the edge of the pool and imagine ourselves doing it, and feel how it feels. You imagine yourself doing it right on, perfectly. Then go out there and do it. Doing a lot of imagery was the major difference in our preparation last year, not just the duet, but also the compulsory figures. About half an hour before we actually did a competition routine we would go through the routine once together on dry land doing the movements. The two of us would do the movements, moving our arms, and feeling the moves while the tape was playing our music.

With performance imagery your ultimate goal is to draw on all of your senses to feel yourself executing skills perfectly. This allows a slight firing of the neural pathways that are actually involved in the performance of these skills. It can be viewed as a way of programming your circuits. What you are trying to do is to program a positive performance into your brain and nervous system so that you will free your body to follow. Imagery helps to establish a positive performance pattern. It also can strengthen self-confidence and help you believe that you can perform in the real situation, in the manner of which you are capable. Quality mental imagery, combined with quality physical practice, increases your overall effectiveness and brings you closer to your dreams.

The earlier you can begin your imagery training, the better. I recall a very talented 8-year-old gymnast who was capable of incredibly clear imagery. She first began mental imagery completely on her own with no knowledge that it was practiced by many great athletes. She would lie in bed at night running through her routines. For her it seemed a natural thing to do. She was able to see the people around her, feel the moves, and experience the emotions.

I remember a 19-year-old university basketball player who had been experiencing difficulty with a particular play in games. I asked her to try to imagine herself executing the play properly and driving in for a successful lay-up. She closed her eyes and sat quietly for a couple of minutes. When I asked what had happened in the imagined scene, she said she had seen a bunch of *X*s and *O*s on a chalkboard going through the pattern of the play.

Contrast this with the vivid mental imagery that Bill Russell was doing when he was 18 and that he discussed in his book, *Second Wind* (Russell, 1979). Russell became one of the best all-time basketball players, winning 11 NBA championships as leader of the Celtics.

> Something happened that night that opened my eyes and chilled my spine. I was sitting on the bench watching Treu and McKelvey the way I always did. Every time one of them would make one of the moves I liked, I'd close my eyes just afterward and try to see the play in my mind. In other words, I'd try to create an instant replay on the inside of my eyelids. Usually I'd catch only part of a particular move the first time I tried this; I'd miss the headwork or the way the ball was carried or maybe the sequence of steps. But the next time I saw the move I'd catch a little more of it, so that soon I could call up a complete picture.
>
> On this particular night I was working on replays of many plays, including McKelvey's way of taking an offensive rebound and moving quickly to the hoop. It's a fairly simple play for any big man in basketball, but I didn't execute it well and McKelvey did. Since I had an accurate vision of his technique in my head, I started playing with the image right there on the bench, running back the picture several times and each time inserting a part of me for McKelvey. Finally I saw myself making the whole move, and I ran this over and over. When I went in the game, I grabbed an offensive rebound and put it in the basket just the way McKelvey did. It seemed natural, almost as if I were just stepping into a film and following the signs. When the imitation worked and the ball went in, I could barely contain myself. I was so elated I thought I'd float right out of the gym. Now for

the first time I had transferred something from my head to my body. It seemed so easy. My first dose of athletic confidence was coming to me when I was 18 years old. (pp. 73-74)

Russell involved himself in the very vivid mental replication of a skilled athlete executing a fast-moving play on the court and driving in for the basket; then he acted out that image. Later he began to create many of his own moves in his mind and played them out on the court.

Developing Your Imagery Skills

If you have never done any systematic imagery training, start with simple, familiar images or skills. For the next week or two set aside 5 minutes a day, either before going to practice or before going to sleep, to work on your imagery. Let yourself relax. Shut your eyes. Not yet! First read the next few sentences. Try to imagine the place where you usually train . . . what it looks like, how it smells, how it feels when you walk in, the people there, the first things you usually do to warm up, the look and feel of the playing surface and the equipment that you use in your sport. Try to imagine and feel yourself doing some very basic skills in your sport— for example, easy running, free skiing, dribbling, passing, throwing, rolling, swinging, turning, moving freely. Through imagery, gradually increase the complexity of the skills as well as the amount of time you practice. As a general rule you should get into a pattern of doing 10 to 15 minutes of quality imagery every day. Most of our Olympic and world champions do at least 15 minutes of imagery daily, and many regularly do an hour or so each day when preparing for major competitions.

In addition to helping you perfect physical skills, imagery is an exercise in concentration. You must create and control the images in your mind. It's a mental exercise and it's tiring, especially in the beginning. So take your time and move into it gradually. It's better to try for short periods of high-quality imagery than longer periods of low-quality imagery.

Keep in mind that your ultimate objective is to experience the image with all your senses. When perfecting performance skills through your imagery try to call up the feel, not merely something strictly visual. The more vivid and complete the feeling, and the more effectively you perform within that image, the greater your chances of replicating this image in the real situation. With daily practice your imagery skills will improve immensely and your images will feel very real, just as some of your dreams feel real.

A good way to perfect feeling-oriented imagery, so critical for excellence in sport, is to actually move your body while doing the imagery. Instead of lying down, get into the normal starting position for the skill.

For example, a kayak paddler can sit with knees bent and arms up as if holding a paddle, and then actually move her arms through a paddling motion as she images and feels her perfect execution in her mind and body. An alpine skier can assume a standing position, leaning slightly forward with knees flexed and arms forward, as if in the starting gate with poles planted. In imagery he then feels himself skiing the course while actually bending his knees and partially moving his body, as if he were actually doing his perfect run. In the quiet of his own apartment a baseball player can stand up, step into the batter's box, see the windup, swing an imaginary bat, and feel the pop of the ball as he imagines and feels his perfect swing. A basketball player can move his body and feel perfect shots, beautifully handled passes, and the perfect execution of a variety of offensive and defensive skills.

When you are doing imagery, beginning the actual movement of the activity often helps you call up the total feeling associated with that movement. An experienced gymnast can run through a complete floor routine with feeling by imagining the moves as she walks across the floor doing slight arm movements, body gestures, turns, and pauses. By combining imagery with real movement, you can speed up and enhance the learning process. As you become skilled at *feeling* imagery, the sensations associated with the movements will surface naturally when you imagine your skills, even while you lie completely still in bed.

As you learn to use imagery to perfect old skills or acquire new ones, something else that you may find helpful is to carefully observe others who do those skills well. Watch an accomplished athlete perform a skill, and as she is doing it, try to feel yourself doing it with her. Do this several times in a row; then try to replay the skill in your own mind, feeling yourself do it. You can use this technique during practices or competitions, or while viewing videos.

I once used a film of a world champion sprinter to help a promising young athlete get the feel of blasting off the blocks and driving through the finish. She watched the film, trying to feel herself go with the image, and then imagined herself moving the same way without the film. She attempted to replicate this feeling of speed, and the specific actions, during her own workout on the track.

The best athletes I work with use imagery primarily as mental preparation for training and competition, as well as for skill correction. Before arriving at the training site they mentally run through what they want to do and how they want to do it. Just before performing important skills, they imagine themselves doing those skills perfectly, and after errors they imagine themselves making the appropriate corrections before repeating the skills. In preparation for competitions they mentally run through flawless performances. They often imagine themselves in the competitive arena—

with the sights, sounds, temperature, spectators, competitors, and coaches—and then focus in on their own performance.

Some of our Olympic champions have even put a clock on their imagery to ensure that their timing and pacing are exact. For example, in preparation for the 1984 Olympic Games Alwyn Morris, gold medalist in canoeing, and Alex Baumann, double gold medalist and world record holder in swimming, did timed imagery. Alex Baumann commented:

The best way I have learned to prepare mentally for competitions is to visualize the race in my mind and to put down a split time. The splits I use in my imagery are determined by my coach and myself, for each part of the race. For example, in the 200 individual medley, splits are made up for each 50 meters because after 50 meters the stroke changes. These splits are based on training times and what we feel I'm capable of doing. In my imagery I concentrate on attaining the splits I have set out to do. About 15 minutes before the race I always visualize the race in my mind and *see* how it will go. I see where everybody else is, and then I really focus on myself. I do not worry about anybody else. I think about my own race and nothing else. I am really swimming the race in my mind. I go up and down the pool, rehearsing all parts of the race, imagining how I actually feel in the water. I try to get those splits in my mind, and after that I am ready to go. I started imagery in 1978. It has been refined more and more as the years go on. That is what really got me the world record and Olympic medals.

You can also use mental imagery to learn new routines, plays, or patterns, and to familiarize yourself with a particular competition site, course, or track. In sports like alpine skiing, auto racing, cross-country running or skiing, and equestrian events, internalizing the course is very important. Our best downhill skiers use imagery extensively to learn the course so that they will be confident in knowing which way to turn when they run the course at 80 miles an hour. During the course inspection they essentially memorize the course by running it through their mind over and over again. Once all the critical landmarks are known, they imagine themselves skiing the course, seeing and feeling what they will actually experience during the race. Without this mental familiarization process, the danger would be dramatically increased, and the confidence a skier needs to really "let it go" in the race would be lacking. Our best cross-country skiers likewise carefully inspect the course, taking note of the difficult parts as well as areas where they can gain ground. This helps them plan strategies and anticipate what they will do at various points in the race (for example, for climbing hills, negotiating sharp downhill turns, pushing limits).

Some athletes find mental imagery helpful to thoroughly evaluate performances and pinpoint important areas for improvement. The process goes something like this: Think of your last competition. Mentally replay what happened just before and during the event. What were you focused on when you were going best? Where was your focus when you were going less than best?

This process can help you become more aware of how your thinking and focus affect you at different points in the competition. It can lead to a more accurate assessment of what you do or what you say to yourself that makes you feel good, perform well, and push your limits. It can also alert you to ways you might be interfering with your own performance and give you specific things to focus on for improvement.

Think about what you can do, or say to yourself, in order to feel better, focus more fully, and perform more closely to your capacity. Then begin to practice focusing this way in training simulations and in your mental imagery for upcoming competitions.

Mental Simulation of Coping Skills

Mental simulation allows you to enter scenes or situations that you can never fully replicate in simulated practice conditions. You can mentally simulate virtually any situation that might arise, or that you would like to approach in a more positive manner, including a coach screaming at you or a stadium filled with 80,000 people. Mentally rehearsing different ways to cope with distractions, competitive anxiety, and negative thinking is extremely important and yet is largely overlooked in the mental readying process. If in your mind you can see yourself, hear yourself, feel yourself, and think yourself through situations in a constructive manner, you will be better prepared to approach these situations the way you would like to approach them in the real world.

Mental simulation lets you prepare for and practice effective responses in your mind *before* you are actually confronted by a real-life problem or distraction. It is a buffered kind of learning that feels real *in your mind* and yet lacks the serious consequences of the failures that sometimes occur in the real world. The mental rehearsal process makes it possible to enter a situation feeling better prepared and more confident.

When you rehearse your focusing or refocusing strategy in your mind, you mentally simulate what you want to do in actual conditions. This in itself can help reduce or eliminate potential problems that might otherwise affect your performance negatively.

When preparing for an important competition you can imagine yourself at the competition site, saying positive things to yourself, relaxing, overcoming critical obstacles in the game, focusing only on the task at hand, pushing your limits, achieving your goals. Whatever you want to do, in sport or outside of sport, you can move a step closer to making it a reality by imagining yourself accomplishing it, step by step.

Pat Messner, a world champion in waterskiing, became extremely anxious during important competitions as soon as she passed the first buoy on the way to the slalom run. When she passed this buoy she'd say to herself, Oh no, here it comes, and a tenseness would overcome her entire body. She decided to employ mental imagery to practice using the buoy as a signal to relax. She imagined herself skiing by the buoy, saying to herself Relax, at which point she would relax her shoulders and think, You're ready . . . just let it happen. This process helped her alleviate the problem in the real situation.

A figure skater complained of becoming extremely anxious in compulsory figures during important international competitions. She was particularly distraught just before starting, when nine judges were on the ice peering over her, and during the first tracing, which followed immediately. She tried to imagine herself at the competition site, from the time she heard her name being called until she had finished tracing the first figure. Merely standing before those 18 peering eyes in imagery raised her anxiety level. As the anxious feelings began to surface, she imagined herself relaxing, focused on her breathing, and said to herself, Nice and smooth . . . flow. She then imagined herself doing the first figure in a calm, controlled, and focused manner. Her major goal was to practice her chosen coping strategy in detail, to feel the effectiveness of her strategy, and to end up focused and in control.

There are many examples of athletes using mental simulation to reduce anxiety, to improve performance, and to cope more effectively with a variety of situations. Some creative uses of imagery were relayed to me by national team archers attending a national training camp. During a workshop on mental preparation for shooting, which I was conducting, I asked the archers about some of the strategies they had been using. A former world champion spoke of how, through imagery, she was able to transport herself to the world championship from her practice site. Instead of seeing the single target that was actually in front of her, she saw targets stretched across the field. She was fully aware of her competitors. On her right was the leading Polish archer, on her left a German. She could see them, hear them, and feel them. She shot her rounds under these conditions in the same sequence as she would shoot in the real competition. She prepared herself for the competition and distractions by creating the world championships in imagery and by actually shooting under mentally simulated world championship conditions.

A member of the men's national team did just the opposite. In the actual competition he was able to mentally simulate practice conditions. As he prepared to draw his bow to shoot his first arrow at the world championships, his heart was thumping. He glanced down at his tackle box (holding equipment and odds and ends) and noticed the words *Go, go, go*, which one of his hometown buddies had painted in red. That note triggered another reality—a flashback to familiar grounds. From that point on in the competition he was at home on the practice range, with one small battered target in front of him. He could even hear some of his buddies on the practice field, chattering and joking in the background, in place of the chatter of many different nations that surrounded him. He shot in a very steady, collected, and relaxed manner, as if he were at home.

In most cases mental imagery is a first step in an attempt to improve certain skills or overcome anticipated problems. It gets you started. It is not very time consuming, and you can do it yourself, wherever and whenever you want. Sometimes mental imagery in itself leads to overcoming a particular problem or improving a performance. The usual sequence, however, is to begin with mental imagery, then practice the imagined skill or coping strategy in a real-world training situation, followed by a simulated competitive situation and finally the competition itself. The examples of the two archers, who combined simulation and imagery, simply point out how you can be very creative in putting together workable strategies.

Advancing Your Imagery

No matter how good or how limited your mental imagery skills are now, you can improve them through daily practice both at home and in your training setting. The more on-site imagery you do in your normal practice environment, the better. If you can imagine and feel the perfect execution of each important skill or program before you do it in training, this will

- force you to focus on what you are about to do,
- remind you of what you need to focus on to do it well,
- improve your imagery skills, and
- set the stage for an improved performance.

Linda Thom, Olympic champion in pistol shooting, commented:

> When I go to the line in training or competition, I mentally go through my shot-plan checklist before I shoot. This strategy started out very mechanically with a physical list of words which I have on the shooting

table, and which I read exactly. These words represented every single step involved in shooting a shot. Then I reduced the steps to key words so that I could go through the list faster. Finally I didn't need a list anymore. I would usually write one word to emphasize what I wanted, such as *trigger* or *smooth*. Then this shot-plan rehearsal became a mix of simple verbal reminders and images, which I ran before each shot.

If you want to develop your imagery to the fullest, you can use my audio-cassette, *In Pursuit of Personal Excellence*. (See the References and Suggested Readings section at the end of the book.)

Chapter 9

□

Relaxation and Activation

**You need a certain amount of tension to be able to go. On the other hand,
if you are too far gone, you just go off the deep end, you lose control.
So it is just being able to find that little narrow comfort zone.**
Steve Podborski

Performers often fail to achieve best performances because they are too "tight," too anxious, too tense, or stressed out. They may end up tensing almost every muscle in the body or totally lose their task focus. Peak performances and personal bests often occur when mind and muscle combine in free-flowing experiences.

Some of the world's best figure skaters have heart rates as low as 60 during their compulsory figures at the world figure skating championships. This state of relative calm undoubtedly contributes to their ability to perform so well—when it really counts, particularly in the figures.

Uptightness and a relaxed, efficient flow do not exist at the same time. Developing the ability to relax your body and calm your mind is important because it allows you to control your activation level and channel your focus, both of which enhance performance. Relaxation procedures not only can relieve anxiety before and during competition but can also lessen postevent anxiety and improve general sleeping patterns.

Individuals have different bodily responses to the onset of stress. Some feel a tenseness in the neck or shoulders. Others experience shaky legs, queasiness in the stomach, a rapid increase in heart rate, sweaty palms, a pounding in the head, and so on. What do *you* feel when you start getting uptight? Stop and think about it! That's a first step to anxiety control. As you become more fully aware of your early signals of stress, you can use them as cues to relax or focus. The trick is to understand your own patterns and to begin to identify and manage them before you get too uptight.

Learning to Relax

To bring on relaxation, some athletes like to focus on relaxing different muscle groups (for example, in the legs, shoulders, arms, or neck) or to focus on breathing slowly and easily, attempting to relax fully with each exhalation. Others like to imagine themselves in a familiar setting with friends or on the beach relaxing as the waves wash gently onto the sandy shore. They may prefer to be alone, talk with others, listen to music, have a massage, seek out a natural outdoor setting; the list goes on. There is no right way to relax. Whatever makes you feel more relaxed and more in control is right for you.

Try to become familiar with different ways of relaxing. Personalize relaxation procedures so that they work best for you. Simple reminders such as *loose, relax,* or *calm* can help relax you instantly if they are well practiced and called upon as soon as you start to feel tense. Self-directed relaxation as well as relaxation assisted by your environment—a long run, a warm bath, a long hot shower, a relaxing jacuzzi, or intimate contact with a loved one—can be helpful in easing you down if anxiety drags on after the event.

Two things happen with effective relaxation. There is a *physiological* relaxation response: Your heart slows down, your breathing slows and becomes more regular, there is decreased oxygen consumption, your muscles become less tense, and you begin to feel a calmness in your body. There is also a *psychological* relaxation response: a shift in focus to something other than that which caused the increased tension in the first place. Your focus may shift from thoughts about how you are "scared shitless," "out of your league," or "going to blow it" to thoughts of your relaxed breathing, the movement of your rib cage, the sensation of specific muscles relaxing, a feeling of calm, the quieting sounds of a song, the beauty in the scenery around you, the pleasant sensations of relaxation, or your overall readiness to meet a personal challenge. In short, your focus shifts from fear of failure, fear of rejection, and worry about terrible consequences to either relaxation or another more constructive focus. The shift away from self-evaluation and worry itself renders you less anxious, and the focus on allowing yourself to relax enhances the reduction in tension.

I remember one athlete saying to me while going through a relaxation exercise in my office, "I don't need to relax in here, it's out there that I need it." It is out there, when the stress begins to build, that we all need it. However, if any coping strategy is to be effective under high-stress conditions, it must be well learned and practiced. You must be able to plug in that response in the space of one deep breath. To be able to do this you have to practice—first under low-stress conditions, then under medium stress, and finally under high-stress conditions. To ready yourself for the competitive arena, you must take advantage of all the stressful situations that you face, so that you'll be practiced at responding effectively. Then you will be ready out there when you need to be.

If you take the time to learn to relax effectively, you will become more aware of your body's internal environment and more able to adapt to your external environment. It is one way to put yourself more in control.

Relaxation for Individual Needs

In my consulting work over the past 15 years, I've heard a number of athletes express a desire to be able to clear their minds and relax more completely for a variety of purposes:

- To fall into a deep and restful sleep, especially before an important competition or when adapting to a foreign environment
- To clear the mind and relax the body in preparation for a quality performance
- To calm down and conserve energy the night before or the morning of an important competition
- To open the mind and body to confidence-enhancing thoughts
- To speed recovery and revitalize the mind and body between events
- To prepare the mind and body for quality performance imagery or healing imagery

As a result of those athletes' requests, and with their guidance and feedback, I developed a relaxation tape that they judged to be effective for their individual needs. It's about 10 minutes long and consists of three parts, each designed to free the listener to enter a complete state of relaxation: muscle relaxation, relaxed breathing, and relaxation through imagery. The script for the tape is reproduced in the appendix. You can make your own tape from this script or listen to my cassette, *In Pursuit of Personal Excellence*, which includes this relaxation script along with five other mental training exercises.

By design this relaxation exercise is shorter than most; contains more variety in approach; and does not include any tensing of muscles before they are relaxed, a commonly recommended procedure developed initially by psychologists for nonathletes. The omission of muscle tensing reflects the athletes' preferences. I have found that, compared to the general population, athletes are amazingly in tune with their own bodies and muscles. Because of this connection they know where their muscles are, can relax them quickly, and generally do not like to first contract a muscle group before relaxing.

Many athletes find it helpful to listen to this relaxation exercise every day, either between workouts or before going to sleep at night, at least until they feel confident in their ability to tune into the body and completely relax. At that point some athletes continue to use it regularly; others use it only when they are facing stressful situations or having sleeping difficulties. Decide for yourself under what circumstances and for what period of time the exercise can be most useful.

Whether you use my relaxation tape or follow your own relaxation sequence, try to get totally absorbed in the feeling of relaxation so that you can recall that feeling in the future.

If your goal is to develop your ability to call upon a relaxation response on your own, in a more stressful setting, then conclude each relaxation session by repeating to yourself a cue word, such as *relax*, *calm*, or *loose*, every time you exhale. This is meant to strengthen the association between your cue word (relax) and total relaxation in your body. Then, without using a tape, begin to think of your cue word and recall the feeling of relaxation. Let the feeling flow quickly through your body. The process goes something like this.

Think to yourself: *relax*, *calm*, *let go*, *loose*. Let that peaceful, relaxed sensation spread through your body. Then scan your body for any areas of tension. Some people find it helpful to imagine a beam of light scanning their body. The light beam is charged with relaxation, so if any area of tension exists, you simply zap it with a beam of relaxation.

Experiment with this process first in a quiet setting, and then start to do it in other settings. In the beginning you may need a couple of minutes to feel completely relaxed. Your goal is to be able to bring on a relaxation response within a few seconds.

Try using your cue word to relax while sitting, standing, walking, running, talking, reading, driving, in school, at work, at meetings, at workouts, and so on.

You can start right now. Breathe in . . . breathe out . . . say to yourself, re-lax . . . re-lax . . . re-lax. Now scan your body for any areas of tension. Are your shoulders relaxed? Is your jaw relaxed? These are often good checkpoints. Zap any area of tension with a beam of relaxation. Set a goal for yourself to relax on the spot five times per day over the next 3 days. You've already done it once today—four more to go. Next, start plugging your relaxation response into potentially anxiety-provoking situations. If competition has resulted in unwanted tension, then begin to simulate competitive conditions in practice and use your cue to relax. Move from simulated conditions to actual competitive conditions, from less important competitions to more important ones. This allows your on-site relaxation response to become well learned and practiced for those times when you need it most.

Taking an exam, participating in a tryout, speaking in class, getting a shot, going to the dentist, having an argument, responding to a customs official, and being stopped in a radar trap—all provide valuable practice opportunities. As soon as you detect any of your personal signals of tension, take a deep breath, exhale slowly, and think to yourself, Re-lax, calm. With practice this in itself can bring on a relaxation response. It is not likely that relaxation alone will eliminate anxiety entirely in a highly stressful situation, but it should help you reduce it to a manageable level and allow you to regain a more constructive focus.

Relaxing Through Exertion

When Florence Griffith-Joyner blitzed the women's 100-meter world record in 10.48 seconds at the 1988 Olympic trials, she commented, "The 10.60 [run in the first round of the competition] made me realize if I continued to concentrate on what I'm doing and stay relaxed, my times would continue to drop." And they did!

Sue Holloway, following her 1984 Olympic silver medal performance kayaking in pairs, spoke of the importance of relaxing:

Almost every 3 seconds or so toward the end I'd have to say, relax, and I'd let my shoulders and my head relax, and I'd think about putting on the power, and then I'd feel the tension creeping up again so I'd think about relaxing again, then power, relax. . . . I knew that in order to have that power I had to be relaxed. You can be powerful but tense, and the boat won't go. You windmill and you stay on the spot and dig yourself into a hole. I wanted to feel the power, the boat coming up, lifting and going. Crossing the line, the thing I remember was just letting the emotion go and being able to say, "That's it, it's over!" I just knew that we'd gone our very hardest.

At first glance, exertion and relaxation may seem to be a contradiction in terms. However, most peak performances in sport occur when athletes feel loose and relaxed in the process of extending themselves. When Larry Cain paddled at a blistering pace to win Olympic gold in 1984, there was a definite sequence of reach—power—relax with each stroke. He extended his limits, but he also paddled relaxed. With top runners you see a similar sequence of stretch—power—relax accompanying each stride. They often speak of running "relaxed" after shattering world records. When you watch cheetahs run at speeds approaching 80 miles an hour, you see that they also run with beautiful, relaxed power.

To further develop and refine the important skills that allow you to relax during exertion, set a goal to work on this during training sessions, and then remind yourself to relax while you are going hard in training. Think of on-site reminders that might help you get into a relaxed but highly focused channel (for example, loose—powerful; power—relax; reach—pull—relax; stretch—grab—relax). Experiment with calling on reminders at appropriate times before and during workouts. In activities that involve repetitive sequences, reminders can be timed to go with the flow of the activity.

Marathon runners would not be breaking personal barriers by running 26 miles in times ranging from 2 hours and 6 minutes to 2 hours and 10 minutes unless they were stretching, pushing, reaching, and relaxing through their limits. The best distance runners run relaxed, breathe steadily and consistently, relax muscles with periodic exhalation, scan muscles for tension, and focus on localized relaxation of tense areas. They contract only those muscles required, relax nonessential muscles (for example, jaw and shoulders), and relax working muscles in the recovery stage to conserve energy and run more efficiently.

By relaxing, and by focusing on specific functions within your own body, you can effect physiological changes in your muscle tension, blood pressure, respiratory rate, blood flow, body temperature, and even your rate of recovery or healing. When attempting to direct such changes, clearly visualize the part of the body that you want to influence, then feel the desired change taking place. There is a specific exercise for directing your own functions toward your own healing, on my cassette *In Pursuit of Personal Excellence* (see p. 186 for details).

When top gymnasts do difficult strength moves like the iron cross, they contract only those muscles that are required to do the skill. (If you tried an iron cross you would probably contract almost every muscle in your body; even your face would be scrunched up.) They execute strength moves with a totally relaxed expression because it is unnecessary and inefficient to contract nonessential muscles like those in the neck, face, and legs. You must learn to relax your nonworking muscles while other muscles are working hard and to relax your working muscles when they are not working—for example, in the recovery phase of sequential movements. You will do this effectively only if you focus on it in training. You know where all those muscles are; you simply have to practice tuning into them and telling them what to do at critical moments.

Charging Bulls

A Chinese coach once said to me, "You can jump over a very high fence when a big bull is chasing you." He meant that being pumped up or charged helps you achieve greater heights. This is often true, as long as you channel that energy in the right direction. But in your haste, you wouldn't want to fall before you reach the fence or run into it rather than going up and over. I have seen athletes become too complacent or under-activated in practices or in low-priority competitions, but I have rarely seen this in important or challenging competitions.

Most athletes are naturally "up" before important competitions and don't require anything additional to heighten their precompetition activation. If they do need a lift it will likely be when fatigue begins to set in, when they are dead tired, toward the latter part of the game, race, or performance. This is when a charging bull or another effective way of energizing may be helpful.

What seems to work best in times of low activation or fatigue during competitive performances is a shift in focus *away* from the fatigue to reminders that help you perform better technically—*reach, extend, follow through*—or to cue words that help you feel energized—*strong, go, charge, power, push, flow, quick, explode.* For some activities these cues can be repeated in a rhythmical fashion; for others a single crisp reminder is more appropriate. Another way to energize is to remind yourself of your goal and the importance of achieving it. Tell yourself, There is a lot riding on this; I've invested too much to give up now; It won't kill me; I have to do it; I want to do it. This kind of reminder or flash is best followed by an immediate shift back to a task focus—a focus on what you should be doing now, in the present.

You probably find it easier to get activated for a competition than to relax because the stakes are higher than at practice, and you have plenty of practice at energizing yourself. You regularly have to get up to a certain level for training or simulations or time trials. You are less practiced at moving from a highly activated, precompetition state into a relaxed and flowing performance zone.

To relax in stressful situations, play down the importance of outcome, slow down your pre-event pace, breathe easily and slowly, let your body be free and loose, and focus on your pre-event preparation and only on what you are doing. To heighten your activation or intensity, remind yourself of the importance of the event—how much you have invested, how much depends on the outcome. Move at a faster pace, watch your competitors, increase the speed and physical intensity of your warm-up (for example, run through warm-up drills at game pace, clench your fists, flex the muscles in your entire upper body, slap your thighs, clench your teeth, grunt, yell, scream).

Active power-filled words, thoughts about outcomes, and short bursts of high-intensity activity increase the heart rate and overall activation level. Some actions that can pump you up are: moving at a rapid pace, jumping up and down, making loud noises, aggressive physical contact, listening to loud rock music, breathing rapidly, and doing short bursts of vigorous physical activity at maximum effort.

Getting activated for practices can sometimes present a problem. But setting specific training goals, and thinking about achieving these goals on the way to practice, is enough to keep most athletes motivated in situations where they might otherwise feel bored or unchallenged. Some also benefit from creating competitive situations in practice—for example, competing against teammates or the clock or for score; training with outside athletes; bringing in officials, judges, or spectators. Some of our best athletes use competitions against (easy) opponents as a challenge to meet personal performance goals and an opportunity to simulate their competition plans in preparation for more important events.

Certainly some events, some skills, and some people require higher activation levels than others. For instance, free skating requires a higher level of activation than compulsory figures; an iron cross on the rings requires higher activation than a free-flowing giant swing; putting a shot requires more explosive energy than shooting an arrow; tough player-to-player defense requires a higher level of intensity than shooting a foul shot. It is important to discover the level of activation where you perform your best and to learn to move yourself up or down into that zone at will.

Once you discover your personal performance zone, you must practice getting into that zone so it becomes natural. To know how is not enough; to be able to put it into action and maintain it when and where you need it is the goal. This takes some practice.

Chapter 10

□

Distraction Control

Heart in champions has to do with the depth of your motivation and how well your mind and body react to pressure—that is, being able to do what you do best under maximum pain and stress.
Bill Russell

If I were asked to choose one mental skill that distinguishes the athletes at the top, I would name their ability to adapt and refocus in the face of distractions.

If you want to perform well consistently in training and at major competitions, you must develop the critical skill of distraction control through regular practice. You must be able to hold your best focus in the face of potential distractions, and to refocus effectively to quickly regain the connection if it is broken.

Distractions come from a variety of sources: family members, relationships, teammates, coaches, competitors, scores, officials, media, sponsors, financial and educational concerns, changes in your own performance level, expectations of others, your own expectations, changes in familiar patterns, and your own thinking before, during, and after performances. Distractions are an ongoing part of sport and life.

When you enter competitive situations, many things have the potential to distract you, upset you, lower your confidence, put you in a bad mood or a negative frame of mind, or tempt you to dwell on results. But something becomes a distraction only if you let it distract you. Otherwise it is simply something that happens as you go through your day or your preparation or your competition. You can choose to be distracted by it or not to be distracted, to dwell on it or to let it go.

The most important point is that you don't *have to* let what you normally think of as distractions affect your performance in a negative way. You don't lose your performance skills because of distractions; you let yourself lose the focus that allows you to execute your skills effectively. Someone may say something that you don't like, but you don't have to react by feeling put down, rejected, or out of control. You may be faced with a judgment, rule, or decision that you feel is unfair, but you don't have to let it destroy your performance by becoming angry or depressed. Your warm-up or performance may not go as smoothly as you wish on a particular day; you may find that frustrating, but you don't have to react by putting yourself down or questioning your capacity. There may be disruptions in your normal pattern—such as crowds, delays, incompetent people, lack of personal space, differences in training facilities, accommodations, or food. You don't have to fall into a bad mood and let your positive focus slip away. You may want a certain result more than anything else, but you don't have to react by overthinking, overanalyzing, or worrying about the outcome at the expense of the focus that will let you perform well.

In major competitions, athletes commonly face a multitude of distractions in a short time. If you let yourself react emotionally to all such distractions, you can be mentally and physically drained by the time you compete. In reacting emotionally to distractions by upsetting yourself or worrying, you expend a lot of energy. If you continue to react in this way throughout an event that lasts for a period of weeks—like the Olympics or the world championships—you risk not only becoming exhausted, but also getting sick. Constantly reacting in a stressful way lowers your resistance. This obviously can hurt your performance and add still another stress factor.

When you are faced with additional stress, additional rest is needed. When you are rested you will cope better with stress. It's important, too, to rest *after* you've been stressed. Setting simple daily goals and planning each day so you have some sense of control over what you do is also very helpful in stressful environments.

At major competitions, if you step back and look at distractions from a distance, as I often do, you realize that most of them are little problems that get resolved within a short time. They really aren't worth wasting your emotional energy on.

The following pointers will help you stay on track or get back on track quickly:

- Know that you can perform to capacity even in the face of distractions.
- Commit yourself to remaining positive.
- Focus on doing what will help you stay positive and in control. A strong positive focus protects you from distractions.
- Get yourself into a positive state of mind before the event, and stay focused on your job within the event; then things will flow. Make positive thinking a way of being.
- Look for advantages in every possible situation, even if the conditions are less than ideal. Look for reasons why you can still be confi-

dent, strong, and optimistic. It is useless to drag yourself down or waste energy trying to control things that are beyond your control. Do what you can do—draw out the constructive lessons, and move on.

- Remind yourself that distractions do not have to bother you. You can refuse to get caught up in them. You can let them go. At a competition site things may happen to you that are stupid, unfair, unexpected, or beyond your control, but you *can* control how you react to those things. Why compound the problem by focusing energy on things that are beyond your immediate control or that set the stage for failure?

- Expect conditions to be different at major competitions. Expect a faster pace, a busier place, and more waiting around. Prepare yourself to face these potential distractions in a positive way. Let them go with as little energy as possible. They are not worth your reaction. Let them bounce off you easily.

- Expect people to behave differently at major competitions, even those who normally would be calm, supportive, and understanding. Observe them with interest, but don't take responsibility for their behavior. Look for your own strength. Remind yourself of where your focus should be.

- Know that you can perform well, regardless of distractions.

- Practice getting back on track quickly. For example, when things don't go well in training or you face problems in your life outside of sport, take advantage of the opportunity to practice refocusing into a more positive state of mind.

- Make a real effort to remain positive—to turn bad moods into good moods. Then you will be totally prepared for your most important competitions.

- After a good day or a not-so-good day, be proud of your effort and of what you have done well and draw out the positive lessons. Then start a fresh, new day.

- If you are troubled by negative situations or haunted by self-defeating thoughts, focus on doing the things that are most likely to keep you in a positive frame of mind. Find your own space, regroup your thoughts, focus on realistic personal goals, know that it is not worth wasting energy on hassles or worry, focus on something that is interesting or beautiful, do something that you enjoy. Think in positive, self-enhancing ways. Remind yourself repeatedly that you can change your mood and perspective. Focus on what is within your control. *Get back in control.*

In stressful situations some athletes find it helpful to imagine themselves surrounded by an invisible force field, as you might see on "Star Trek." This force field allows you your needed personal space and shields you from intrusions or potentially harmful input. Negative comments, distractions, or hassles simply bounce off your protective shield as you move toward your goal; only positive things come through.

Your best precompetition focus is limited to preparation for your own performance—something over which you exert control. If you anticipate distractions, you can help yourself by getting adequate rest, increasing your use of positive imagery, and focusing on your own preferred preparation patterns. Remind yourself that your best performance focus centers on what to do and how to do it—not on distractions and not on results.

Think only of what you must do. It has worked well in the past. Bring yourself into this frame of mind: It is the only place to be.

You are not asking yourself to do anything unreasonable—only to perform as you can perform.

The doing is your goal. Execute your task the way it should be done, the way you can do it. Just feel it. Your body cooperates with your thoughts and images when you send a clear message and then just let it happen. Trust your preparation, trust your body. Let it happen by instinct. Focus ahead and go. Let your body lead.

Training to Refocus

Think of a recent situation in training, competition, or daily life where you "lost it"—blew your cool, lost your positive focus, or lost your connection to your performance. Can you rerun that scene in your mind and imagine yourself responding more effectively? You are confronted with the same situation, but you don't let it bother you. You rise above it. It bounces off you with minimal disturbance. You get back on track quickly and pursue your goal. You remain positive, calm, controlled, focused, and effective. Try it.

When you imagine yourself responding more effectively to distractions that you have already faced, you help set the stage for perfecting your refocusing skills. You then have to practice refocusing in the real situation—in the real world.

The next time something goes wrong in training—a negative comment, a missed move, too much thinking, a loss of focus—challenge yourself to turn it around within that training session. Set a goal to regain your focus on total connection to your performance, and to do it as quickly as possible.

The next time you are about to get upset or slip into a bad mood because of your reaction to someone or something, concentrate on regaining a positive focus or a focus that connects you to your task. This is a challenge. If it were easy everyone would be good at at, but few of us are. And we would all perform to our fullest capacity under high-stress conditions, but few of us do. Nevertheless, this is possible if you make this focus your daily goal, and whenever you are successful, make a note of *how* you achieved it.

Sylvie Bernier, 1984 Olympic diving champion, began to work seriously on distraction control about 1½ years before the Olympics. Previously she had suffered in major competitions from distractions that resulted in inferior performances, especially on the last dives of the competition. Sylvie's main distraction was paying attention to the scoreboard instead of focusing on her own dive.

> I started to shift away from the scoreboard a year and a half before the Olympics because I knew that every time I looked at the scoreboard, my heart went crazy. I couldn't control it. I knew that I dove better if I concentrated on my diving instead of concentrating on everyone else. It was harder to get ready for 10 dives than for 1 dive so I decided to stop looking at everyone else, just be myself and focus on preparing for my next dive. That was the best way for me to concentrate for my event. Between dives at a meet, using a Walkman was the best way for me to shut everything out. I knew I could win, but I had to dive well. I stopped saying, "This diver's doing this, so she's going to miss this one," or "If she misses one, I'm going to win."
>
> At the Olympics I really focused on my dives instead of on other divers. That was the biggest change in those 2 years. Before that I used to just watch the event and watch the Chinese, and think, Oh, how can she do that? She's a great diver. I thought, I'm as good as anyone else, so let's stop talking about them and focus on your own dives. That was an important step in my career.

Lori Fung, 1984 Olympic champion in rhythmic gymnastics, discussed the importance in her sport of refocusing between events, especially after an error.

> If you have a bad routine, you've got to get back to zero again. You just have to say, "Okay, that's forgotten. It's totally forgotten." That's it. Go out and do the next one, and pretend that the next one is the first routine of the day and it is going to count. Otherwise, you are never going to pull back again. You can't do anything about it. You can't do anything about the score you're getting. You can't do anything about why you dropped that one move or how great it was; it's over and done with. Sometimes it's really hard to make yourself forget it, but the more you try, the better you're going to get at it in the future.

Lori does a thorough performance evaluation, but she does it at an appropriate time after the competiton—not within routines or between events.

Laurie Graham, winner of many world cup races in downhill skiing, reflected on her way of handling a mistake within a race.

> Once I push out at the start, I am focused on where I am at the time. A lot of it is "line" in downhill. You don't go right at the gate, you've got the line that you have been running all week and you just say, "Okay, I've got to stay high here, I have to go direct here, I have to jump this jump," just so I am aware of each obstacle as it comes. If I make a small mistake, often it doesn't even register for me until the end, when I'm at the bottom. At the time you are still thinking, forward, speed, momentum. You don't carry the mistake down the hill. It is shelved until later. Often those mistakes will mean just running them out, and it really won't cost you that much time if you don't panic, if you just let it turn out and get back on track.

Distraction control is probably the most important skill of all for consistently performing to your potential in your most important competitions. It is a skill that needs a lot of practice to be perfected.

What focus do you want to carry today? Think about it. Make it clear in your mind. See it, feel it, believe that you can make it happen. You have the capacity to make it happen. Take control. *Make it happen.*

Chapter 11

□

Simulation

To be there without ever having been there—that is the goal of simulation.

Simulation training lets you practice your desired performance responses and coping strategies in circumstances that are as real as you can make them *before* you actually take them into the real situation. Test pilots and astronauts were among the first to use simulation training effectively. In preparation for a space voyage, astronauts take great care to simulate countdown, blastoff, docking, touchdown, in-flight and surface activities (complete with low gravitational pull), and possible malfunctions along with appropriate responses for each. The cost of error is astronomical when human life' and billions of dollars are at stake, so no effort is spared to ensure that the astronauts are as well prepared as possible—without yet having ventured into space. Before they leave the launch platform they want to feel totally ready—as if they have been there before—knowing that they can perform well and handle any problems that arise.

In sport, simulation training can help prepare you to more effectively meet the challenges that you will face. Simulation helps you prepare physically through the high-quality, high-intensity training required to replicate the physical demands of competition. It helps you prepare mentally for competition conditions and likely distractions, so that you are better able to stay focused and get the job done regardless of the demands of your event or the happenings around you.

Who Uses Simulation

In the 1988 Winter Olympics, figure skater Elizabeth Manley delivered her best-ever international performance, winning the long program and placing second overall. She previously had experienced problems with her long program and often worried, before competing, about whether she could get through a clean program. To perform to capacity at the 1988 Olympics, she needed to feel confident that she was fit enough to skate the whole program with no problems and to know that she could maintain total focus on executing her skills. To fully prepare herself Liz did more complete run-throughs of her program that year than she had ever done before. In her final simulations, which took place in the Ottawa Civic Center, she imagined that she was skating in the Olympic Saddledome. Liz was very confident going into her long program at the Olympics, and she executed a flawless program. The additional simulations had really helped.

Eric Heiden won five gold medals in speed skating at the 1980 Winter Olympics. Speed skating is a high-intensity sport that involves a lot of pain when you are going flat-out. To excel in a sport like this, you must somehow learn how to push through pain barriers. Toward the end of many events your muscles are hurting, burning, screaming.

Fortunately, the pain experienced by most well-conditioned athletes as they extend limits is simply the sign of a sane body talking to its seemingly insane master: "What are you doing to me? I'm wiped out, my muscles are reaching a point of extreme fatigue. I've had enough pounding for one day. Can't we stop?" No we can't stop, Body. *I'm the master here and we have to continue, but it won't be long now . . . only another few strokes, gates, steps* (or in some cases, miles). *Anyway, it's not actually pain; it's just the feeling you get when your muscles are really working.*

"That's easy for you to say, tucked away up there, sitting safely in your skull. Why don't you come down here and try pushing a little weight?" And so the debate continues. But this is a battle the mind must win over the body because, in many events, you must push past the pain barrier to explore your limits. Most of us can tolerate higher levels of pain or stress while performing well and feeling OK—if we are comforted by the belief that it is helping us, or that we can control it if we choose to or have to.

Eric Heiden often used simulation training and skating imitations to practice pushing through barriers. He even included the pain in his mental imagery of races and raced through it in his mind. He pushed through pain barriers so often in training that he was totally prepared to endure and extend limits in major competitions. Sometimes he pushed so hard in training that his legs were too shaky to stand. Like Eric, speed skater Gaetan Boucher trained with incredible intensity and used simulation training extensively in preparation for his double gold medal performance at the 1984 Winter Olympics. However, it is important to realize that you can't train with that intensity every day or every interval. Even though you need to find ways of pushing limits and replicating competition demands on a regular basis, rest is also essential. You need to be physically and mentally rested to get the best out of yourself in major simulations and major competitions.

It is unfortunate that many skilled athletes perform poorly in competition because of unforseen circumstances that could easily be replicated or simulated during training. When Greg Joy, former world record holder in the indoor high jump, competed in the Sunkist Invitational Track and Field Meet in Los Angeles, his performance suffered from such unforeseen events. Greg, who jumps from the left, requested that the high jump runway be altered to meet his needs. "I called the arena manager earlier in the week and he assured me everything would be arranged, but nothing was done." Greg spent much of his warm-up time trying to convince officials to rework the runway. They didn't. He became upset and proceeded to move the sections himself. "So I didn't get a good warm-up. I was so hyper by the time I was going to jump I was shaking. The PA announcements were also distracting. I didn't have one good jump."

Adverse or unforeseen conditions can be better met and overcome if conditions have already been simulated in practice. For example, Greg might have been able to practice alternate or shortened approaches that would work on less than ideal runways, and then jump well in practice; or practice jumping well after a brief warm-up, a poor warm-up, or no warm-up at all; or practice jumping with PA announcements coming on or people yelling at inopportune times. Greg's physical performance skills were with him at the Sunkist meet as they were in other meets. They didn't disappear. However, they were blocked because he could not focus effectively. You come much closer to tapping your potential if you can enter a scene like the one Greg faced thinking,

> It's unfortunate—but no big deal. I can alter my approach and still perform well. I can perform well with a brief warm-up or even a poor warm-up. I can perform well with PA announcements going on right in the middle of my performance. I'm in control here. I have my skills. All I have to do is focus on doing them.

Performing under simulated adverse conditions is one way of demonstrating to yourself that you can do well under all kinds of circumstances. By foreseeing and working through possible problem situations, you can enter them with much more confidence. Simulation helps you to do what you are capable of doing.

Real-world simulation prepares you to overcome all kinds of potential distractions. Think of the kinds of things that happen or might happen in big meets or important games. Introduce them into your practice setting. Those that cannot be replicated in practice situations can be simulated through mental imagery.

Introduce the expected. Enter the gym or arena, warm up, and play your game or run through your events just as you would in competition. Bring in judges, officials, cameras, and where possible, athletes to compete with.

Run through your event, program, or game in uniform, in the rain, in the sun, in the heat, in the cold, when tired, when fresh, after eating, after missing a meal, in the morning, in the afternoon, in the evening. Practice overcoming difficult offenses and defenses, false starts, someone passing you on the inside late in the run, coming off the bench, coming on strong toward the final three quarters of the race or game even though you have slipped far behind. Introduce sounds of applause or PA announcements just when you are beginning an approach or are halfway through a routine. Warm up on your own and run through your events on your own as if the coach were not there.

Have your coach, close friends, or other athletes introduce some expected "unexpected" events. For example, the coach (or a friend role-playing the coach) can tell you that you have an hour to warm up and then start the competition in 15 minutes; she can change the lineup, offense, defense, or order of events at the last minute; she can bring in judges, unfair officials, important evaluators, cameras, lights, and so on. You can practice being calm, focused, and in control under all these simulated conditions. Before introducing these kinds of distractions, the overall rationale for doing so should be discussed openly among athletes and coaches.

A young figure skater found that, while she was waiting to perform in competitions, she often became aware of other skaters coming off the ice saying, "It is so hot out there . . . it is so hard to get through." As she stepped on the ice herself she worried about the heat and about how it would affect her performance. During the final minutes of her 5-minute program she was thinking, It's so hot . . . my mouth is so dry . . . feels like there's no air . . . I don't think I am going to get through to the end. In her last competition she barely scraped through the last portion of her program and was not at all pleased with her performance. Interestingly, she never worried about the heat in practice meets or exhibitions. It only happened in competitions, even though the physical setup in exhibitions was basically the same: packed arena, bright lights, and high temperature. This led me to believe that the young skater's anxiety about performing well in the heat of competition was raised more by the other skaters' comments about the heat than the heat itself.

We discussed the possibility of practicing with an elevated arena temperature. This posed some logistical problems, so we decided to try increasing the skater's body temperature and leaving the rink manager's body temperature alone. We agreed that, at the next practice, she would dress very warmly in heavy clothing and then try running through her full free program.

She reported back a few days later and said, "I did my program in practice with a big sweater and leg warmers. I was burning hot, but I didn't have a problem with it. I didn't even think about it." From that time on, heat was no longer a major problem in her competitions. Even if all the other skaters came off the ice complaining about the heat, she was never preoccupied with it. She really just needed to know that she could handle the situation without a problem—which she could. The simulation merely provided a little confidence-enhancing proof.

Many athletes would like to have more confidence in their ability to do what they think they are capable of doing. Many would like to enter competitions knowing they will get through their routines or perform to their capacity. Competitive simulation helps build this confidence. Athletes sometimes find it helpful to take on more in their simulations than they do in their competitions. For example, if you know that the competition will require you to do 1 routine on a particular apparatus, do 1 routine in practice and then repeat it immediately; if you know you will have to do 6 routines in one day, do 12 in practice; if you know that one 5-minute skating program will be required, do two in a row; if you know that your game will last an hour, play an additional half hour of high-intensity overtime.

Obviously you must build up your performance level by setting progressively more difficult goals, and you must be well rested on the days that you choose for these kinds of simulations. However, once you are used to doing more than is required, doing what is required is no big deal. If you are accustomed to playing four or five periods of fully focused high-intensity hockey in simulated competitive games, you should be able to enter the competitive situation with full confidence in your ability to focus and endure the mere three periods. Top gymnasts have used this approach successfully. I have seen them execute two complete routines in a row before dismounting. This is one reason their routines are so flawless in competition. The knowledge that in practice they regularly do more than the competition demands gives them full confidence that they can "hit" clean routines.

You are in the best position to determine what kinds of simulated conditions might be most helpful in your sport. The important point is that, if you have been exposed to most of the expected and unexpected conditions that are likely to occur at major competitions, you will be better equipped to stay focused and to perform your best under these conditions. If you have practiced doing more than is required, you will feel more prepared. You will know you can do well. No sweat. Well, some sweat—but you'll know you can nail it. Simulation gives you added confidence in your ability to do what you set out to do. It helps you believe in yourself, and that is crucial in all sports. Your objective is to reach the point where you can face all kinds of challenges or distractions and still have confidence in yourself to come through. You want to know that your capabilities are there—no matter what! This frees you to actualize your potential and to do so much more regularly.

Emulating Others

Following the positive examples set by others is another form of simulation. You attempt to emulate another person, such as a highly respected or focused athlete, by replicating that person's positive attributes. You consciously set out to borrow selected positive attributes from others in an attempt to improve yourself. Sometimes when I see, meet, or get to know someone, I discover in that person something that I really like or admire. It may be a physical or a psychological attribute. I think, I'd like to move that way . . . to be open in that way . . . to handle my problems like that . . . to express my feelings the way she does . . . to use my time that way . . . to be relaxed like that . . . to carry myself that way. . . . I really like the way she approaches competition . . . copes with losing . . . exudes confidence . . . hustles on the court. . . . I like his style of jumping, her fast extension, his combination, her dismount. I'm going to try it!

You can look at and selectively draw on other people's strengths in order to better yourself physically or mentally. You can literally attempt to be that person in certain respects, to see how it feels. You can see yourself as that great athlete in stance, in posture, in execution. You can tell yourself, Today I'm going to pretend I'm so-and-so from the time I step on the floor; I'm going to walk tall, the way he does, and try to execute my moves as gracefully; I'm going to be calm just like her, even if the coach starts yelling; I'm going to work really hard just like he does for the whole game. You make a conscious effort to be, or focus, a certain way for a specified period of time. If it feels right and helps you, hang on to it. If not, let it slide.

Some of the best professional impersonators report that they can achieve things while impersonating that they cannot achieve while being their usual selves. For example, they become funnier or more witty or reach a higher pitch in singing than in ordinary life. Emulation is another path to extending perceived limits.

Other people can also be used as a stimulus to avoid behaving in certain ways. You might see a behavior, a technique, or a physical being and say to yourself, I am not going to be like that, perform like that, or act that way. Then do your damnedest to avoid behaving that way.

Role-playing is another method that can help you to prepare for some situations that you face in high-performance sport. Although role-playing has not been used extensively in sport, it lends itself to certain situations. Let's say that you want to be better prepared for media interviews or for interacting with a particular coach, athlete, or official. After thinking about what you want to say or how you want to respond, you can act out your preferred responses while someone else plays the role of the person whom you will encounter. This allows you to practice effective communication in a simulated situation before you actually express yourself in the real situation. Role-playing is much like preparation for a speech, where you first rehearse alone in your room and then try the speech out on a few friends before actually giving it.

Role-playing lets you practice communicating in the manner in which you would like to communicate. It should enable you to respond in a way that will make you feel more at ease in the actual situation. This technique was helpful for an athlete who had left one coach to train with another. She was worried about being confronted by her former coach at an important competition. I role-played the coach, using some of the things that individual might actually have said or done, while she assumed her own preferred role. After the role-play she felt better prepared for a confrontation, "just in case"; a meeting with the coach would not catch her off balance and thus interfere with her performance. The coach never did confront her, but she felt ready—and that feeling of readiness for a potential distraction enhanced her overall mental readiness for the competition.

In some cases an athlete may want to voice a concern or a suggestion to a "feared" coach; role-playing might allow for better communication. Some athletes have also used role-playing in preparation for speaking before a group. In this application a few people might pretend to be the audience (some sleeping, some looking attentive) while the athlete assumes the role of the speaker.

Role-playing has been used very successfully in helping athletes prepare for meetings with the media. Several Olympic teams with whom I have worked used this approach before the Olympic Games. Pre- and postcompetition interviews and a press conference were simulated, with one athlete playing herself and other athletes acting as press people. The "press" managed to raise some excellent questions, as well as some that were uninformed or tasteless—like those with which athletes sometimes are confronted. Each team member had a chance to think about, and practice, asking questions and responding to them. The exercise turned out to be fun, as well.

Success Through Simulation—A Case Study

Indonesian athletes were world champions in badminton for an unprecedented number of years. They have a history of winning when it counts. I have watched them play; talked with them, their coaches, and their former world champions; and visited their training camps. One main reason they were on top of the world so long is their extensive use of simulation training. They simulate every aspect of the game (for example, strategy, coming from behind, bad calls, high temperature, crowd effects), particularly for the world championships.

Strategy. Long before the match, the Indonesian players know everything about their opponents—their strengths, weaknesses, playing style, technical peculiarities. They study films on their opponents and gain from the experience of teammates who have already faced them. They preplan a strategy and mentally run through exactly what they will do when their opponent does A, B, or C. Teammates sometimes role-play the actions of opponents in simulated games. They know where they should return the bird for a particular opponent before they play him, and they prepare to place the bird accordingly before it ever reaches them in the actual game.

They also practice anticipating their opponents' returns, which means knowing beforehand where the bird will likely go and planning to be there. If this strategy works on 7 out of 10 shots, it is worth targeting the anticipated return area. In a sport like badminton, speed is closely linked to anticipation. The player must anticipate and move toward the return area before the bird is fully hit, particularly in a hard smash. This situation is similar to a hockey goalie facing a slap shot. To be successful he must anticipate where the puck will go and be there before the player makes full contact with the puck. The puck moves from the player's stick to the goal faster than a player's capacity to react; anticipation is therefore essential. By studying where the puck or bird usually goes under various conditions or with various opponents, a player can greatly increase the chances of being in the right place at the right time. There is no doubt that the Indonesian players are quick, but they have much more than speed: They know where and when to move. They are almost always in the return area before the bird arrives, even on blistering shots in doubles play. Their speed is well directed, their opponents' shots are well anticipated, and their own strategies are well practiced through simulation training.

Coming From Behind. Top players build confidence in their ability to come from behind and win a game by simulating such situations in practice. They may start a game at 14 to 3. A stronger player will begin with 3 or 4 points and a weaker player with 13 or 14 points. The objective for the stronger player is to come back and win the game. For the weaker player the objective is to prevent this from happening, or at least to have some strong rallies. With a proper matchup, both players can play hard and the stronger can come back to win. This process gives less experienced players a chance to play the champions and lets the champions practice coming from behind. For many years in the Thomas Cup

Championships, whenever the Indonesian players did fall behind, they were consistently able to come on strong to win. The fact that they were behind did not seem to fluster them at all; they had practiced coming back. They knew they would come back and they did. Top wrestlers have used a similar strategy to teach athletes to fight back from a near pin. A stronger wrestler allows a weaker opponent to get him into a position where he is almost pinned, and his objective is to come back from this difficult predicament.

Bad Calls. Poor officiating—for example, calling a shuttle out of bounds when it is obviously in bounds—is simulated in practice to prepare players to overcome the frustration that can follow a bad call. The purpose of simulation is discussed, and it may then be implemented in practice games as well as in exhibitions. Sometimes the simulating "official" makes a series of bad calls. The player's goal is to ignore bad calls and focus on preparing for the next point, to shift focus from something beyond his control to something within his control. There were no emotional outbursts or even second looks from the Indonesian players after questionable or close calls at the championships. They simply got on with the game.

High Temperature. For many years the Thomas Cup Championships have been held in Jakarta under extreme temperature conditions. The outside air temperature in the evening is in the mid-30s Celsius (mid-90s Fahrenheit), and the humidity is in the 90s. The arena is packed with 12,000 sweaty people, and there is no air conditioning. In addition, there are heat-producing television lights right next to the court, and all windows and doors are closed to prevent the drift of the shuttles. Needless to say, it is hot! The spectators end up dripping just sitting in the stands.

How do the Indonesian players prepare for these conditions? They prepare by living and playing in the heat and by bringing in large crowds to fill extremely hot and humid arenas for exhibition matches. If visiting teams are to play to capacity under such extreme temperature conditions, they must also prepare for them. The best preparation is to practice and play exhibition games for a couple of weeks in the same time zone, in a similar climate, under similar conditions and then rest well for the tournament. This prepares an athlete to walk into that arena and feel totally prepared to go the distance.

Crowd Effects. I never heard a crowd roar as loudly as the crowd in Jakarta for the badminton championships. It was deafening, and it was a very partisan crowd. They heckled opponents and roared approval for their heroes' every shot. The fact that a lot of private betting is associated with these games may explain some of the fans' enthusiasm. In some countries a crowd of 12,000 people for a badminton match is unheard of; in Indonesia it is normal. The audience would be even larger if the seating capacity in the halls were greater. Younger players learn to adapt to these crowds by growing up with them. The junior championships attract 8,000 fans. In addition, national team members travel throughout the country giving exhibitions to large crowds. They invite the public to the main badminton hall in Jakarta for simulation matches in final preparation for the championships; the free invitation is accepted gratefully, and the hall is full. This final simulation is aimed at readying the athletes to walk onto the championship court feeling totally prepared mentally.

The Indonesians often undertake more in their training than is required for their championships. For example, they may play 1½ to 2 hours straight at a very fast pace. They may play whole games where one player is allowed only to lob or smash, or play defensively, or play to the backhand, while the other player can use all his moves. To keep the pace moving, to work on speed, and to develop anticipation, one player may play against two opponents, or multishuttle games (developed by the Chinese) may be introduced. In multishuttle games it is possible to play nonstop badminton— with a shuttle always in play— or to practice reacting to shuttles coming rapid-fire from all corners of the court.

As a result of training for more than is actually required on the day of the competition, the players are in superb physical condition. They use their fitness to their advantage, particularly in extreme temperature conditions. They can maintain a very fast pace or deliberately keep a rally or game going a long time, simply to tire out their opponent.

A former world champion and one of badminton's all-time greats believes that following three simple rules, which can easily be applied in practice simulation, gives a player an advantage both strategically and psychologically:

1. Never stop a game to change a bird when you are winning.
2. Never change a serve if it is working.
3. Never change a shot (for example, playing to the opponent's backhand) if you are scoring.

It is interesting to note that, while still competing, the Indonesian superstars work with the most promising junior players. The reigning and longtime world champions in both singles and doubles spend about 2 days a week coaching and playing with younger players. The youthful players have an opportunity to play with their heroes, to watch them at close range, to learn from them, to follow their actions, and to be inspired by them. The championship players also gain from the exchange and enjoy it very much.

If you want to become a champion, train with the best. If you are already a champion, let younger athletes train with you so that you can help them in their pursuit of excellence.

The only country where I have witnessed in-depth simulation training that equals or surpasses that of Indonesia is China. In table tennis, a sport that the Chinese have dominated since the mid-1950s, they use simulation extensively and in some very creative ways. In the early 1980s some of the high-quality simulation procedures used with their best table tennis players were being applied in badminton. In the latter 1980s China became the dominant badminton power in the world, defeating Indonesia.

The Chinese are masters of the art of simulation. It has played a major role in their traditional martial arts (wushu) for many years and more recently has been applied in many contemporary sports such as badminton, volleyball, gymnastics, and diving. With their most successful teams the Chinese go a step beyond other countries in the extent to which they repeat skills or programs in training (extrasimulation). They prepare athletes to perform when fatigued and to meet specified opponents. For example, some skilled Chinese athletes are trained to replicate the playing styles of opponents from other countries so they can provide simulation training for national team members. Such training strengthens athletes' overall readiness to face the challenges of high-level competition as long as adequate rest time is allowed and individual differences are respected.

Chapter 12

□

The Zen Approach

Man is a thinking reed, but his great works are done when he is not calculating and thinking. Childlikeness has to be restored with long years of training in the art of self-forgetfulness. When this is attained, man thinks yet he does not think.
D.T. Suzuki

One of the most intriguing aspects of sports and the arts as they were originally practiced in Asia long ago was their focus on training the mind. Zen was developed and experienced through the martial arts and the fine arts, but its ultimate purpose was for the living of life itself.

For me one of the most important lessons of Zen is the concept of *oneness*, a concept that was also promoted by many of our aboriginal people. It means becoming inseparable from the essence of what you are doing at each moment you are actually doing it. It is being all here, totally present and absorbing yourself in, connecting yourself to, and becoming one with your body, your task, nature, the tree you are looking at, the child you are playing with, the person you are talking with. When you are in the process of *doing*, in a sense you become what you are doing and suspend all judgments about yourself, others, or your performance. When you begin to reflect, deliberate, question, or judge along the way, you lose your connection or become judgmental, apart from, separate, tentative. The original natural bond between mind and mind, mind and body, mind and task, mind and creation, or mind and nature is broken. There are times for thinking and reflection, but there are also times to connect totally with what you are doing and to leave your thinking behind. Performance is a time for connection rather than reflection.

Transcending Technique

I often wondered how the great fencing masters prepared for duels in the old days, before the time when touches were recorded on an electronic scoreboard. How did the great swordsmen prevent themselves from becoming too focused on outcomes and suffering a fatal performance flaw when the stakes were literally life and death? Many overly anxious swordsmen did not live to tell their tale, but what of those who survived and continued to excel?

Daisetz T. Suzuki, in his excellent book *Zen and Japanese Culture* and his introduction to the book *Zen in the Art of Archery* (by Eugene Herrigel), touches eloquently on this question. Suzuki discusses the connection between Zen and the ancient art of swordsmanship as follows:

> If one really wishes to be master of an art, technical knowledge is not enough. One has to transcend technique so that the art grows out of the unconscious. . . . You must let the unconscious come forward. In such cases, you cease to be your own conscious master but become an instrument in the hands of the unknown. The unknown has no ego-consciousness and consequently no thought of winning the contest. . . . It is for this reason that the sword moves where it ought to move and makes the contest end victoriously. This is the practical application of the Lao-tzuan doctrine of doing by not doing. (Suzuki, 1959, pp. 94, 96)

For a swordsman to excel or even survive, he had to free himself from all ideas of life and death, gain and loss, right and wrong, giving himself up to a power that lives deeply within him. In essence he had to clear his mind of all irrelevant thoughts and trust his body to lead.

The swordsman who performed at the highest level of excellence was likened to a scarecrow that "is not endowed with a mind, but still scares the deer" (Suzuki, 1959, p. 100).

"A mind unconscious of itself is a mind that is not at all disturbed by effects of any kind. . . . It fills the whole body, pervading every part of the body . . . flowing like a stream filling each corner." If it should find a resting place anywhere, it is a state of "no thinking," "emptiness," "no-mind-ness" or "the mind of no mind" (Suzuki, 1959, p. 111).

Juan Belmonte, the great Spanish bullfighter, reflected on the moment when he first freed his body and mind to perform.

> All at once I forgot the public, the other bullfighters, myself, and even the bull; I began to fight as I had so often by myself at night in the corrals and pastures, as precisely as if I had been drawing a design on a blackboard. They say that my passes with the cape and my work with the muleta that afternoon were a revelation of the art of bullfighting. I don't know, and I'm not competent to judge. I simply fought as I believe one ought to fight, without a thought, outside of my own

faith in what I was doing. With the last bull I succeeded for the first time in my life in delivering myself and my soul to the pure joy of fighting without being consciously aware of an audience.

Canadian Olympian Kim Alleston spoke of a similar phenomenon.

I have experienced flow on several occasions, and to me it was a feeling of separating my body from my conscious mind and letting my body do what came naturally. When this happened things always went surprisingly well, almost as if my mind would look at what my body was doing and say, Hey, you're good. But at the same time not making any judgments on what I was doing because it was not "me" that was doing it; it was my body. This way, by not making any judgments, it was easy to stay in the present.

Olympic figure skater Charlene Wong and Olympic downhill skier Kellie Casey have done exceptionally well at drawing on some aspects of the Zen perspective to free themselves in their quest for personal excellence. When Charlene is able to "turn on her autopilot" a wonderful program unfolds. When Kellie suspends conscious thinking and "lets her body lead" she has a great run. For the duration of their best performances, they both suspend critical evaluation and trust the body-mind connection to work without interference from or clouding by conscious thought.

In the ancient art of swordsmanship, focusing was intimately connected with life. "When a stroke is missed, all is lost eternally; no idle thinking could enter here." A consciousness too occupied with irrelevant thoughts and feelings stands in the way of "successfully carrying out the momentous business of life and death, and the best way to cope with the situation is to clear the field of all useless rubbish and to turn the consciousness into an automaton in the hands of the unconscious" (Suzuki, 1959, p. 117).

Inhibitions created by distracting thoughts or emotions could result in a swordsman's failing to see or detect "the movements of the enemy's sword with the immediacy of the moon casting its reflection on the water" (p. 133). Seeing and instantaneous action of body and limbs are essential. This is no place for minds obscured by irrelevant thought or clouded by anxiety. No obstruction should come between mind and movement.

As one Japanese Zen master pointed out, you can read the environment much more clearly when you are "calm internally," just as you can see the reflection more clearly on a calm lake than on a disturbed one. Anxiety is like wind that disturbs the image on a calm lake.

Suzuki points out that

the perfect swordsman takes no cognizance of the enemy's personality, no more than of his own. For he is an indifferent onlooker of the fatal drama of life and death in which he himself is the most active participant. . . . The swordsman's unconscious is free from the notion of self. As soon as the mind "stops" with an object of whatever nature—you cease to be master of yourself and are sure to fall victim to the enemy's sword. (pp. 96-97)

Suzuki goes on to say than an idea, no matter how worthy and desirable in itself, becomes a disease when the mind is obsessed with it. The obsessions the swordsman has to get rid of are

1. the desire for victory,
2. the desire to resort to technical cunning,
3. the desire to display all that he has learned,
4. the desire to overawe the enemy
5. the desire to play a passive role, and
6. the obsession to get rid of whatever obsession he is likely to be infected with (pp. 153-154).

"When any one of these obsesses him, he becomes its slave, as it makes him lose all the freedom he is entitled to as a swordsman." Whenever and wherever the mind is obsessed with anything, "make haste to detach yourself from it" (p. 154).

The following quotations from Yagyu Tajima, the great 16th-century Japanese swordsman, provide some eastern visions to reflect upon:

- Emptiness is one-mind-ness, one-mind-ness is no-mind-ness, and it is no-mind-ness that achieves wonders.
- Give up thinking as though not giving it up. Observe the technique as though not observing.
- Have nothing left in your mind, keep it thoroughly cleansed of its contents, and then the mirror will reflect the images in their *is*ness.
- Turn yourself into a doll made of wood: it has no ego, it thinks nothing; and let the body and limbs work themselves out in accordance with the discipline they have undergone. This is the way to win (pp. 114-115).

A fencer with whom I worked got me thinking about performing without thinking and without thinking about not thinking. He combined some aspects of oriental and western psychology to improve his fencing performance. He developed a precompetition plan that helped him start in a more calm and relaxed state. What he wanted most was to compete in a Zen mind-set. In the beginning he wrote out a list of quotations that triggered in him the primary feelings of a Zen perspective. They included the following.

Primary Set of Feelings for Zen Mind-Set

1. Zen is against conceptualization. The experience is the thing. Verbalism often becomes an empty abstraction.
2. If you want to see, see right at once. When you think, you miss the point.
3. When I look at a tree, I perceive that one of the leaves is red, and my mind *stops* with this leaf. When this happens I see just one leaf and fail to take cognizance of the innumerable other leaves of the tree. If instead of this I look at the tree without any preconceived ideas I shall see all the leaves. One leaf effectively stops my mind from seeing all the rest. When the mind moves on without stopping, it takes up hundreds of leaves without fail.
4. To think that I am not going to think of you anymore is still thinking of you. Let me then try not to think that I am not going to think of you.
5. Do not rely on others, nor on the readings of the masters. Be your own lamp.
6. You have mastered the art when the body and limbs perform by themselves what is assigned to them to do with no interference from the mind.

The fencer read these quotations to himself several times before competing, as a reminder of the state of mind that he sought. He had some initial success but also some subsequent difficulty in maintaining this approach throughout his most crucial bouts. He refined his approach into a series of key words (for example, It, it . . . be with it. Be here . . . be all here), which he plugged in whenever he experienced too many thoughts or too much anxiety. As he went out to compete he began to tell himself, You're here to fence and nothing beyond the experience of fencing really matters . . . just go out and fence and enjoy yourself. When he was able to follow these simple reminders, his body took over and he moved in an incredibly fluid way—sometimes making touch after touch without thought. After bouts like this he occasionally found himself wondering where all those great moves came from.

The fencer could not always enter this state, but it began to happen more frequently with more tournaments. He began searching for competitions in order to practice improving his mind-set and letting his performance flow. Improving his overall perspective toward competition was his primary goal, but he also found help in backup strategies, such as verbal reminders and relaxation, when he ran into problems. A Zen orientation is not something that can be accomplished hurriedly, but it is certainly responsive to nurturing, as the fencer's comments make clear.

For the first few competitions, after reading and talking and thinking, I realized that I was too focused on what was wrong in the bout. I paid attention to what was wrong. To turn that around, I got back into the doing. I went into one tournament thinking, There's nothing that says I have to be tied up in a competition. The first two bouts were great, then I started to tie up. I couldn't let go of the feeling. I was first able to turn it around by becoming interested in everything around me, instead of being too worried about the expectations of others. This took a bit of time. I had to be *in* the competition. With each subsequent competition I had better and better control for more and more of the time. The coach stayed away and let me work things out for myself. Telling me technical things at the last minute, or after I'd blown something, just made things worse. I thanked him for staying quiet.

When speaking about his last competition the fencer said,

As I stepped up for the bout, I thought, I am here for the fencing . . . nothing else matters . . . get into the experience. At no time did the thought of winning or losing enter the picture. I got into the finals, which was my goal, and we won the team competition. The "pressure situation" didn't faze me. On one occasion one guy did upset me emotionally. I went into the corner, did some relaxation, read my Zen reminders, came back, and won a key match 5 to 0. My primary strategy worked fine and I gave myself reminders in the bout (for example, I'm here to experience it.). Many people commented on how relaxed I was. I really enjoyed myself and beat four good fencers. I was there to fence—that's all.

He ended our discussion by saying, "The *event* is the focus. If I focus on the event, the feeling comes automatically. So I just let my interest get absorbed in the event. I relax and enjoy it. Lots of hits are unintentional. The guy just runs into my point."

Certain things cannot be forced. You must free yourself to let them happen. You don't have to *try* to be happy. You simply live and experience the simple joys of life, and happiness comes as a by-product. In similar vein, you don't have to consciously *try* to win in order to win. During the contest you simply get absorbed in the experience; "be" in the present, trust your body, allow the performance program that has been ingrained in your mind and body to unfold, and the winning takes care of itself.

Chapter 13

□

Self-Hypnosis in Sport

Belief is the mother of reality. Excellence is a state of mind.

One way to turn more of our life dreams into reality is through self-hypnosis, a state of relaxed receptivity that can release some of the untapped potential within each of us. My father, Dr. Emanuel Orlick, has worked in the area of hypnosis and self-directed mind control for over 60 years. I am thankful that he consented to share his perspectives on hypnosis by writing this chapter.

The Power Within

Humans everywhere are looking inside as well as outside themselves, seeking to develop or utilize talents, abilities, or powers that they feel they possess. No matter how excellent you are, you can be better. This is true for all of your mind-body attributes, talents, and abilities. No matter how good any of these may be now, they can be better—*much* better.

Of all the methods that I have used to unlock the doors to the powers within each of us, one stands out, and that is hypnosis. We don't know what hypnosis is any more than we know what electricity or magnetism is. However, I do know what hypnosis can do for you and how you can use self-hypnosis to awaken and tap the fantastic mental and physical powers lying dormant within you.

All of us have within us amazing mind-body powers that are sometimes brought into play when we face life-and-death situations. Almost every newspaper has on file eyewitness accounts of people who have performed incredible feats of strength in dire emergencies. For example, all of the major news media carried reports of a 110-pound mother who lifted the back of a station wagon off the crushed legs of her screaming 17-year-old son after a jack slipped and he was trapped beneath.

We all live and function far below our maximum mental and physical limits until something of sufficient importance triggers the use of our dormant mental and physical powers. Somehow, hypnosis and self-hypnosis can act as this triggering mechanism, thus enabling ordinary humans to perform superhuman mental and physical feats. With practice, each of us can boost our normal, everyday mind-body levels much higher than they are now.

Vasili Alexeev, one of the all-time greatest Soviet weight lifters, was able to tap into his own mind-body potential. Before each lift he appeared to enter a trancelike hypnotic state. You could feel his intense concentration penetrate your own mind as he stood over the ponderous barbell at his feet, preparing himself mentally to thrust it over his head. You had the feeling that it was not only muscle power but some form of psychic energy that enabled Alexeev to lift those enormous poundages and break one record after another.

Hypnosis or self-hypnosis substitutes one powerful, positive, dominating thought for a number of distracting, competing, negative thoughts; it substitutes one powerful, positive belief for a number of competing negative beliefs; it substitutes one powerful *I can* for a number of competing *I can't*s; it suspends a host of "normal" critical, doubting, restraining, interfering thoughts and focuses all of the relevant mind-body faculties on the accomplishment of one goal to the exclusion of all competing goals. Perhaps the simplest way to describe the focusing aspect of hypnosis is to compare it to a magnifying glass that can concentrate ordinary, harmless sun rays so strongly into one narrow point that they burn a hole through a piece of paper.

Under hypnosis babies have been delivered, teeth pulled, and operations performed, without pain and without drugs; metal rods have pierced through tongues, cheeks, and muscles, with no pain and no bleeding; feats of strength and memory recall have been performed beyond known capacity; psychic abilities (for example, ESP) and self-confidence have been strengthened; healing has been accelerated and diseases cured. If an individual is able to perform an extraordinary feat under hypnosis, then he or she must have possessed the capability of performing it before going under hypnosis and should be able to perform it *without* going under hypnosis.

Enhancing Performance

Hypnosis, self-hypnosis, suggestion, and autosuggestion all have the capacity to enhance human performance.

Hypnosis occurs when a hypnotist places a subject in a relaxed, receptive state, which can range from very light to very deep. In this state the normal critical faculties of the subject's conscious mind are, in varying degrees, temporarily suspended, and the subject thus becomes very receptive to the hypnotist's suggestions.

In *self-hypnosis* the subject acts as his own hypnotist, putting himself into the relaxed, receptive state just described. Thus, the subject becomes receptive to any strong or repetitive suggestions he makes to himself, either directly or indirectly. Under self-hypnosis the subject may talk to himself, read previously prepared scripts or listen to prerecorded scripts, or may listen to scripts being read by another person. In self-hypnosis the subject controls everything, from start to finish, in each session.

Suggestion is a process in which one person directly or indirectly influences the thoughts or actions of another in the normal waking state. For example, a parent can strengthen a child's confidence by regularly calling attention to her capabilities in a positive way. Advertising, too, is suggestive because it strives to influence the thoughts and actions of others. Thus, television advertisements, which impact on both the visual and auditory receptors, can condition viewers to buy pills that are touted to relieve those headaches that the ads help to create.

In *autosuggestion* the individual directly or indirectly influences her own thoughts or actions in the conscious, waking state. Autosuggestion can be intentional or unintentional and may have positive or negative effects. An example of positive autosuggestion can be seen in Muhammad Ali's constant repetition of the phrase, "I am the greatest." His use of this phrase and his subconscious belief in himself played a major role in his rise to become one of the greatest boxers ever and in the length of time he stayed at the top.

Both positive autosuggestion and self-hypnosis can help you in your sports activities. You can use autosuggestion by reading short scripts over and over again; by repeating positive phrases to yourself whenever your mind is not otherwise occupied; and by playing recorded suggestions to yourself as you drive to school, work, or training, or at any other time.

Think of your brain as a highly sophisticated computer that you program to direct your body in a certain way, as the space center computers direct an unmanned vehicle to land on Mars. Your body is the vehicle, your brain is the computer. Once the brain is programmed, your body must follow its commands, must seek out the goals you have established, and must strive constantly to achieve them. You are the programmer, and you determine what you will feed into your brain.

Think of your ultimate goal. This goal must be etched into your neuron pattern so deeply and so strongly that you will do everything in your power to achieve it. You must believe, with every fiber of your being, not only that you can achieve it and must achieve it, but that you will achieve it. I have never met a person who was a success at anything who did not believe in his or her ability to succeed. Unfortunately, most of the people around us, including our own families and coaches, spend more time telling us what we cannot do than what we can do. Therefore, your first step is to instill in yourself an unshakable belief. For some people there is no quicker, easier, more permanent, or more effective way of doing this than through hypnosis or self-hypnosis, fortified by suggestion or autosuggestion.

Through hypnosis your normal critical, judgmental, or negative thinking can be suspended temporarily, so that the highest possible degree of absolute belief can be inculcated rapidly. Once the belief becomes a permanent part of your subconscious thought process, you will automatically behave in accordance with this belief.

Simple Steps to Self-Hypnosis

The secret of self-hypnosis is twofold: (a) you must fixate your conscious attention, and (b) you must relax your body. The moment you do these two things you are actually in self-hypnosis. Pick a spot on the wall in front of you right now and stare at it while you let your body become limp and relaxed. Keep staring and relaxing for a few moments, and you will feel yourself sinking deeper and deeper into self-hypnosis.

That is all there is to it. Even in this very light hypnotic state, you can begin to program yourself with beneficial positive suggestions. Anyone can put herself into self-hypnosis simply by fixating her conscious attention and relaxing. With practice you can go deeper and deeper and the programming will become more and more effective. Even in the lightest state of hypnosis you can accomplish remarkable things, such as eliminating the pain of a throbbing headache, curing insomnia, improving your concentration, and so on.

The remainder of this chapter is aimed at helping you fixate your conscious attention, relax your body, and make your subconscious mind more and more receptive to the beneficial positive suggestions that you will make to yourself. Once you are in a relaxed, receptive state, then the most important thing is repetition. Whether you are programming yourself for the first time, reprogramming yourself, or reinforcing past programming, it is important that you repeat each positive suggestion many times to implant it deeply and firmly in your subconscious mind.

Four Steps to Follow

Effective self-hypnosis involves fixation, relaxation, receptivity, and repetitive suggestion.

Fixation.   It really doesn't matter on what you fixate your conscious attention. However, one of the most effective objects is either a candle or a black dot in the middle of a piece of white paper. Any piece of white paper will do, and the black dot can be any size you wish. I usually use an index card on which I draw a circle with the help of a dime and then fill in the circle with a black marking pen. This gives me a focus point on which to concentrate my attention. I have found that I get the best results when this card is placed about 12 inches away from my eyes and a little above them. Also, I prefer to face a blank wall, preferably dark, with the light coming from somewhere behind me.

Relaxation.   Over the years I have developed my own method of relaxation, which I believe is the easiest and most effective for use in hypnosis. I call it the "think into" method because you must *think into* your various body parts to make it work. You may have some difficulty thinking into some body parts the first time you try it, but after a few attempts it will be extremely easy. Try it right now. Let your mind run through your body from your head, down your left side, through your left leg, into your left toes. Let your mind scan your left toes as if it were an X-ray machine. Try to feel the existence of these toes. If touching the toes of your left foot helps your mind make contact with them, by all means reach down and touch them. Then try to feel the existence of these toes without touching them. Keep doing this until you have no difficulty *thinking into* the toes of your left foot.

Repeat the whole process with the toes of your right foot, again doing everything in your power to force your mind to recognize the existence of your toes. Do the same thing with other body parts and soon you will be able to think into any body part, muscle group, or internal organ, quickly and easily. It helps if you can visualize each specific muscle or body part. Some people learn this technique more quickly if they first look at an anatomy chart to see exactly what it is they are trying to visualize. This is particularly true of the less well known internal organs.

To facilitate relaxation when you are about to induce self-hypnosis, it is helpful to follow a specific sequence, starting with your toes, working your way up your body, and ending with your fingers. After a few practice sessions you will be able to do the whole procedure from memory, without referring to the instructions that follow. At first it will take a few minutes as you read and think into the body parts listed, but before long you will do it in a matter of seconds.

The sequence is as follows:

1. *Think into your toes.* Let your mind scan your toes like an X-ray machine. With your mind, command your toes to Relax! Relax! Relax!

2. *Think into your feet.* Let your mind scan your feet like an X-ray machine. With your mind, command your feet to Relax! Relax! Relax!
3. *Think into your calves.* Let your mind scan your calves like an X-ray machine. With your mind, command your calves to Relax! Relax! Relax!

Repeat exactly the same think-into sequence for your thighs, buttocks, abdomen, lower back, chest, upper back, shoulders, neck, face, arms, hands, and fingers.

After you have followed these instructions three or four times, close your eyes and do the sequence from memory. Start with your toes and work up your body as described, and finish with your fingers. You should have no difficulty following the sequence. It is not necessary to cover every body part mentioned. The important thing is to reach the major segments of your body and the muscle groups that activate them. Your subconscious mind knows these much better than you consciously do, and once it starts it will automatically think into all of them.

Receptivity.   Fixation and deep relaxation lead to a state of receptivity for positive suggestion. With practice you will be able to enter this state more completely and more quickly, until the time comes when you will be able to relax instantly just by saying to yourself, Relax! Relax! Relax! Not only will this increase your receptivity to self-hypnosis, but it will help you eliminate undesirable stress and tension whenever the need arises.

Repetitive Suggestions.   To develop the greatest possible control over your body and yourself, prepare a short script to read, to think to yourself, or to play back on tape a number of times when you have put yourself into the relaxed, receptive hypnotic state. Your self-suggestions can relate to any area in which you would like to improve. Your script should be short, powerful, and positive. Repeat the script three times. The most effective procedure is to first use repetitive self-suggestions during self-hypnosis and to follow this up with autosuggestion during the event itself. Following are three sample scripts, with pointers for their use:

Sample Script: My tremendously powerful brain has absolute control over all of the cells, tissues, and organs that make up my entire body. It has complete control over all of my feelings, emotions, and reactions. If I feel the jitters coming on I will simply say to myself, Relax! Relax! and the jitters will vanish.

Repeat this script to yourself a number of times during each self-hypnosis session until it becomes implanted deeply and firmly in your subconscious mind. Then, whenever you do feel the jitters coming on and want to control them, just repeat the words, Relax! Relax! and they will vanish.

Sample Script: I am an outstanding hockey player. I have everything it takes to score goals. Whenever I shoot at the net I will think and look directly at the best piece of open space and shoot the puck directly into that space. I will shoot and score. I will shoot and score. I will shoot and score.

When sitting on the bench, during a practice or a game, you can reinforce the script through autosuggestion. Repeat to yourself, I will shoot and score. I will think and look and shoot at the best open space. I will score goals. I will think and look and shoot at the best open space. I will score goals.

Sample Script: I enjoy running. I am in great physical condition and I am improving every day. I have a very powerful brain and body. When I run, my brain and body combine their power to speed up the flow of oxygen and nutrients to my hard-working muscles. They work in complete harmony to speed up the removal of waste products from my muscles. I am strong and efficient.

While running you should visualize the oxygen and nutrients flowing to your working muscles and visualize the waste products being removed from your working muscles. While running, you should also repeat the words *Relax, Relax* to yourself, thinking into your arms and legs and other working body parts. This will encourage better relaxation between the vigorous contractions and speed up recovery between each thrust, thereby helping you increase your running efficiency. As you begin to feel your body extending itself, say over and over to yourself, Strong and efficient . . . strong and efficient . . . I could run forever.

Whatever you want to accomplish, you must think it, see it, feel it, and do it.

The evening before you enter any event, no matter how unimportant it may be, you could choose to use self-hypnosis to do your very best. Think to yourself, I will perform my best; I will perform to my capacity. Imagine yourself doing your best and finishing the way you want to finish.

On the day of the event, for which you have prepared properly, think and say to yourself over and over again, I feel great! I feel terrific! Today I am going to run the best time I have ever run! As you repeat these positive thoughts to yourself, make yourself feel great, make yourself feel terrific, and really do your utmost to run the best race you have ever run. Believe it and do it.

Getting Started

You now have the information you need to put yourself in self-hypnosis and to begin to use this power to draw out and develop all of your mental and physical capabilities.

Select a quiet room where you can complete your entire self-hypnosis session without being disturbed.

Place your focus object—a candle or a white card with a black dot—in front of the place where you will sit, making sure that it is about 12 inches away from your eyes and a little above them.

Place your scripts or other self-programming materials (for example, tapes, tape player) on a table just in front of your chair. If you have memorized your script or know exactly what you want to program into yourself, so much the better. Sit down on a fairly comfortable chair facing your focus point. Get yourself into a receptive state.

Place your forearms on the table with the palms of your hands facing down.

Think relaxation. Think of every muscle in your entire body becoming soft and limp.

Stare at the black dot on the white piece of paper (or the candle).

Take a fairly deep breath, hold it for a moment, and then let it out slowly. As you exhale, say to yourself, Relax! Relax! Relax! Repeat this breathing and exhaling process seven times, letting your entire body become more limp and more relaxed each time.

Your eyes will begin to water. Then they will blink and your eyelids will get heavier and heavier until it is all you can do to keep them open. The moment your eyes begin to blink, or water, or close, you will know that you are sinking into the receptive state of self-hypnosis. A tingling sensation in your hands or fingers is another indication. Don't worry about being sure you are under or how deep you are under. If you follow the steps outlined here, you will be receptive to your own self-suggestions.

If you want to sink still deeper, then say to yourself, I am sinking, sinking, sinking, deeper, deeper and deeper. Repeat this a number of times and then say to yourself, I am now in a deep, deep, deep state of self-hypnosis, and I am sinking deeper and deeper and deeper. You must see yourself sinking deeper and deeper; you must feel yourself sinking deeper and deeper; you must really believe that you are sinking deeper and deeper; and you will sink deeper and deeper.

After taking your seven fairly deep breaths, start your "thinking into" sequence, beginning with your toes and ending up with your fingers as described earlier. Do this mentally with your eyes closed; command each body part, as you scan it with your mind, to Relax! Relax! Relax!

By the time you reach your fingers you should be in a very relaxed, self-hypnotized, receptive state, and you may proceed to feed the desired suggestions directly into your powerful subconscious mind. Do this by opening your eyes and reading your prepared script. Before doing so, be sure to tell yourself that you will remain in the relaxed, receptive hypnotic state even after you open your eyes. If you have taped your script, you may open your eyes, switch on your tape player, and then close your eyes again. Or you can have a close, trusted friend or teammate turn on your tape or read the script to you when you are in the hypnotic state. If you are alone without a tape, it may be best to first memorize your script and to then simply repeat the suggestions to yourself as you fall into the hypnotic state.

At the completion of each self-hypnosis session, while you are still in the very relaxed, receptive state, say to yourself, When I hold my next self-hypnosis session, I will be able to enter a deep state of self-hypnosis quickly and easily.

Finally, just before you are ready to wake up, say to yourself, When I count three I will wake up, and when I wake up I will feel great, I will feel terrific, I will feel better than I have ever felt before. Then count one, two, three, and wake up feeling rejuvenated.

If you go to bed immediately after your self-hypnosis session, sleep will come rapidly and the powerful suggestions that you have just given yourself will become even more deeply entrenched in your subconscious mind.

When you awake next morning, say to yourself, I feel great—I feel terrific—and you really will. Think it! Believe it! And act accordingly.

For more detailed information on self-hypnosis for sport, or for specific self-programming scripts developed by Emanuel Orlick, see the References and Suggested Readings section.

Chapter 14

□

Making Your Strategies Work for You

Man cannot discover new oceans unless he has courage to lose sight of the shore.
André Gide

You now have at your disposal some of the major means to mental control and excellence. If you experiment with some of these approaches, your options for personal growth will become clearer and more individualized. But you must act upon knowledge for it to be of real value. You have to experience strategies to understand them and to discover how they can be most helpful for you. This means practicing an approach or coping strategy long enough, and often enough, for its effects to surface in a consistent and natural way. Even when no visible signs of improvement are immediately evident you are often laying the foundation for future personal growth.

Persistence

Part of the challenge of pursuing excellence is to be persistent in pursuing your goals and to continue to accept yourself throughout the growth process. When you apply specific self-growth strategies to your personal situation, expect improvement, but don't expect instant miracles. For example, if you've been highly anxious in competitive situations for years, don't be disappointed and give up on a strategy if you are not totally calm by tomorrow. Although I have witnessed dramatic—literally overnight—improvements, improvement is more often a progression. Take it step by step, day by day, moment by moment, and *be persistent*. You will have ups and downs in mental training just as you do in physical training. Sometimes you will feel mentally strong and totally in control; other times you may temporarily slide back into less constructive ways of thinking and thereby upset yourself or underestimate your potential. But you will roll back into control. With persistence you will be focused and in control more and more of the time.

I deliberately use the term *persistence* rather than effort. With some approaches, persistence involves noneffort rather than effort. Did you ever try to go to sleep and end up tossing and turning for what seems like hours? You keep telling yourself, I *have to* get to sleep, try to go to sleep. Then as soon as you stop trying so hard, you slip away effortlessly into slumberland. In some cases noneffort, or less conscious effort, yields results that forced effort continually chases away. You can achieve some things more readily by "trying easier," by taking your time or moving toward your goal in an unhurried way.

Persistence means giving something enough time to work. Don't be too quick to say, "I tried that and it didn't work." How long did you try it? How long did you practice it? How fully did you focus on it? Did you gradually introduce the strategy, first in a relaxed setting and then under more stressful circumstances? Did you give yourself enough time to allow the feeling, or focus, to surface naturally without rushing for instant results?

Often when a self-growth strategy does not work, it is because of a lack of persistence in its application. For example, trying to refocus for 1 minute and saying it doesn't work is like training for a competition for 1 minute and claiming that it doesn't work. The 1 minute may not work, but the training does. The fact that an attempt doesn't work immediately is no indication that it will never work. Imagine if you had approached the refinement of physical skills in that way! How skilled would you be today?

It is true that some strategies will not be compatible with you, and you should not waste time on them. But if you do select a strategy that seems right—even a little bit right—give it a chance to work for you.

Remember these points when first introducing a new approach for self-growth or mental control:

- Go with what seems workable for you.
- Don't overload yourself with strategies; start with one or two.
- Try the approach in practice situations until you sort things out.
- Come up with a cue word to help bring the response, or focus, into effect (for example, *focus, power, flow, control, relax*).
- Practice using your cue word as a way into your desired mental state.
- Before the event think of the way you would like to feel or focus in the event, and remind yourself of the perspective you want to carry.
- Let that feeling surface freely.
- Prepare a backup strategy in case the feeling doesn't surface.
- Give your chosen strategy or strategies a chance to work.
- Expect improvement but not overnight miracles.

- Be willing to lose a little in the short run to gain a lot in the long run.
- Remember that experimentation and refinement are necessary for progress and perfection.

When you are introducing new strategies, or before they are well practiced, you may think too much about what you are thinking or about what you are supposed to be thinking. A female fencer commented:

In the first two bouts of the tournament I was thinking so much about what I was thinking that I didn't fence. It took losses in those two bouts for me to realize what was happening. I was expecting everything to just happen and it didn't. Once I started to concentrate on fencing my opponent, things slowed down, I began to relax, and I won the next two bouts. The latter two wins were against much stronger fencers than the first two losses.

During the event, focus on the doing. A cat pursuing a mouse is not thinking about what she should be thinking about. She is focused on the doing. The purpose of your strategy is to get into that focused frame.

The best time to evaluate or to think about what you have thought about is after the event, unless an immediate change in strategy is required within the match. In this case a brief evaluation and refocusing can occur at some break in the action—after the touch, point, or match. If thinking begins to interfere with your focus during the event, change channels by focusing on something concrete or physical that will get you back on track.

The process of learning to improve your focus, control your anxiety, or change channels is in some ways like learning to stand and walk. You may wobble or fall lots of times before you become fully stable, balanced, and in control. You need the same kind of persistence to walk and run with your mental skills as you do for your physical skills.

Goal setting may help you become more persistent, as will charting and monitoring your progress, keeping a daily log, writing yourself reminders, and rewarding yourself for steps along the way. However, for any of these techniques to really work, you must want to improve your focus, your performance, your health, or to grow as a person. No one can force you to *want* to grow; this is a decision that must come from within yourself. Once you have made the decision, persistence does not guarantee that you will achieve your ultimate performance goal; it does guarantee that you will grow along the way. It's the journey that gives life its meaning—not necessarily the arrival at a distant destination.

Part III

Overcoming Obstacles

Preceding page: Mary Fuzesi, top 10 finisher at age 14, rhythmic gymnastics, 1988 Olympics, Seoul.

Chapter 15

□

Preventing
Panic Situations

**Nobody hands you excellence on a silver platter. You earn it through
planning, preparing, and persisting in the face of all obstacles.**

Preparing for a major life event or an important performance is like preparing to run a wild river. You must first take stock of the difficulties and then plan an appropriate course. When you choose a particular course, do so for good reasons. Know what you will do to get back on course if the current pulls you off course. Know this even before you start out. If you must change course in midstream because of some unforeseen obstacle or opportunity (for example, an opening), be alert and adaptable enough to do so. If one strategy does not work, implement another. In case you should capsize, be well practiced at recovering, so that all is not lost. The price of lacking a backup strategy on a wild river may be going over a falls. To avoid potential problems, heed these reminders:

1. Look the obstacles over and become familiar with them.
2. Plan a suitable course (your major strategy).
3. Plan a backup strategy, in case a problem arises.
4. Run your course through your mind.
5. Get in and go.
6. Remain alert and ready, eyes wide open and body reacting.
7. Don't fixate on one obstacle too long or you will be unprepared for the next.
8. Perceive the obstacle, but don't let your mind stop with it.
9. Continue to move forward, making use of your obstacles, your position, and the flow of things around you.

If you begin to implement solutions before problems get out of hand, you will experience less distress and better results. This is like taking steps to prevent a headache from cropping up, or introducing a remedy at the slightest sign of onset, instead of waiting until your head is pounding out of your skull; or feeding a baby at the first sign of hunger, not waiting until the infant is in a screaming rage. Ideally you anticipate and prepare to solve potential problems before they arise.

If you wait until a situation is totally out of control, or until you are in a panic, it becomes much more difficult to implement an effective solution. However, if you catch things as they are surfacing (Hey, cool it, relax, eat, drink, focus), you have a much better chance of regaining control quickly and staying in control.

So, when you know that you will be entering a situation that has produced anxiety in the past, prepare yourself mentally and physically (for example, have a long run or do some relaxation exercises) so that you begin in a calmer state. Even if your anxiety level does begin to rise as the event approaches—and it probably will—you will end up in a calmer state because you started in a calmer state.

Planning Your Psychological Path

Performing your best when it counts most requires that you focus on doing what works best for you. This is easier to do if you develop a precompetition and competition plan, along with a series of prepracticed solutions to potential problems. Basically you have to know what you are going to do before you do it. You need to know that you are going to use a particular focus or strategy because it has worked for you, and you need to know what to do if it does not work.

To be as prepared as possible, and to experience as few distractions as possible, many top athletes develop an *on-site psych plan* and a personal *refocusing plan*.

Your on-site psych plan is your precompetition and competition plan. It is a detailed account of the sequence of events you will go through from the time you arrive at the competition site to the time you finish your performance. Your refocusing plan is a list of potential problems or distractions that could arise and your proposed means of coping with each.

Completing Your Psych Plan

Three questions (what to do, why do it, and what to do if it doesn't work) should be thought out, responded to, and practiced in detail long before the event. A fourth question (How did it go?) lets you assess your effectiveness in implementing your plan and should be answered after the event.

What to do. Think about the exact procedure you would like to follow from the time you arrive at the competition site to the time you finish your event. List your preferred preparation activities in the actual sequence in which they will occur. Use the sample plan, below, as a guide if you'd like. Some athletes prefer and gain from very detailed descriptions of activities, thoughts, and behaviors. Others prefer more of a sketch to remind

Sample On-Site Psych Plan
Event: Track Sprinter

What to do	Why do it?	What to do if it does not work?
General warm-up: long slow stretching	To feel loose, relaxed, and calm	More stretching, "relax," reminder—can run well no matter how warm-up feels
Event preparation: keep warm, active, stretch periodically until event time	To stay loose	Extra sweat suit, run loose, relax
Replicate part of race at full speed, short duration but intense enough to sweat	To feel confident in speed	Visualize best previous race—feel it. Then simulate first 20 meters
Simulate start with heat before with cue words	To feel ready for explosive start	Simulate in imagery if not possible physically—think explosive in imagery
See yourself, feel yourself run the way you want to run	As a last minute reminder before letting body do it	Tell yourself how you want to feel and run
Approach blocks: "breathe," "relax," "ready," "alert," "strong"	To feel I'm 100% ready	Remind self of past best, of untapped potential—"I need to feel butterflies, I'm going to run well"
In blocks: ready position, "breathe out," "relax"	To feel everything's under control	Let shoulders relax, focus on breathing
Set position, think "blast off," "blast off"	To fly off the blocks, hard to hold back, fast as lightning	"Explode, uncoil," "spring like a cat"

1. How did it go?
2. Any changes required in plan for next time?

them of their major focus or job, while some simply review the general perspective they want to carry and let it unfold. Whatever the approach you intend to follow, it should be well practiced. Your on-site psych plan should be practiced in mental imagery, in a practice setting, in a simulated event, and then in a real-world event. Your procedures and proposed strategies should be automatic (or almost automatic) by the time you implement them in an important event.

Why do it? After you have outlined your basic activities, procedures, and strategies, think about why you are following each of them. What do you expect to get from each, in terms of your feeling or performance?

What to do if it doesn't work. Suppose that a procedure or strategy does not work the way you would like it to, or that it does not work at all. Then what are you going to do? Think about it and find a backup strategy. Backup strategies are called into play only if the original strategy is not doing the job. For the most part backups will remain in reserve, but it is important to know that you can call on them if you need them.

How did it go? When the event is over, assess the overall effectiveness of your plan. What parts went well? What areas need additional work for improvement? Do any changes in focus, procedure, or strategy seem warranted?

Athletes in many sports have gained from personalized on-site psych plans. Every world champion, Olympic champion, and professional champion whom I have worked with or interviewed (and they have been numerous) has developed an effective way of mentally preparing for competition and a preplanned competition focus that he or she has found effective. It is likely that you also have the beginnings of a plan that probably only needs refinement to take you where you want to go.

It is interesting that many athletes who clocked their best performances in high-intensity events were engaged in vigorous physical activity right up until the last minute or two before the event. At that point there was a zoning in, a brief mental review of the best performance focus, and a complete focusing on exploding from the ready position at the "start" signal.

If you think you might benefit from seeing the detailed psych plans of many great athletes in various sports, look at my books *Psyching for Sport* and *Psyched* (see the References and Suggested Readings section).

Making Your Refocusing Plan

At the World Student Games, track athletes were corralled in a cramped holding area for about 30 minutes before being lined up and marched directly from the entrance tunnel to the starting blocks. Their last possible contact with their coach or teammates was more than 30 minutes before the event. At the Moscow Spartakiade, divers were crowded into an extremely small and impersonal waiting area between dives; this gave some of our athletes a feeling of no personal space. As divers on the 10-meter platform prepared for their dives, large flags, strategically placed at eye level, began to move at the other end of the pool. Interestingly, this movement only occurred when visiting divers from top competing nations dove. At the Olympic Games it is not uncommon to face 10 or 15 distractions in the course of one day.

Every athlete should have ready a refocusing plan for potential distractions. To develop a refocusing plan, start by listing the things that *usually* bother you at competitions, followed by other things that *could* bother you. Let's say you are preparing for a very important event that comes along only once or twice in a lifetime. You want to be as prepared as possible to cope with both expected and unexpected circumstances that you may face at this event. Therefore, find out as much as you can about what these events have been like for other athletes in the past; you can learn from former athletes, coaches, films, and articles. On the basis of your own experiences as well as the experiences of others, make an intelligent guess about what the event will be like for you and how you need to prepare for it.

Think about distractions or hassles that have affected you in the past as well as particular things that are likely to happen at your upcoming event. Include distractions that could arise in the week or two leading up to the event; at the training site; at the competition site; on the day of the event; within the competition; between halves, events, or periods; and after the competition. Develop a refocusing plan for these potential problems. Your aim is to avoid as many irritating distractions as possible and to cope well with those that you cannot or do not wish to avoid. You may prefer that no storms blow your way, but if they should come, know how to avoid them or be well prepared to meet them.

You can break your plan into major IF-THEN components:

- IF this happens, THEN I do this.
- IF this doesn't work, THEN I do that.

Plan your strategy in detail. Write down reminders or cue words that will help you do what you want to do. Use the reminders in practices and simulated conditions. Become familiar enough with them to call upon them naturally in problem situations.

If you have practiced "cooling it," slowing or picking up your pace, channeling your focus, refocusing, relaxing, and accepting uncontrollable events, you are less likely to get upset over various kinds of psychological games, changes in training schedules, long waits, coach or media pressures, crowded conditions, regimented procedures, or demanding game circumstances.

Unexpected things will always occur at high-profile events. Although you cannot anticipate every possible adversity, you can prepare an effective on-site coping response to use in the face of almost all unexpected happenings. If you feel yourself starting to react negatively to something unexpected, use these distracting thoughts, or unsettling feelings, as a signal to tell yourself to SHIFT FOCUS! If you repeat *SHIFT FOCUS* several times in a row, it will generally break you away from the distracting thoughts long enough to refocus on something more constructive.

The whole coping sequence might unfold as follows: SHIFT FOCUS—SHIFT FOCUS—SHIFT FOCUS. This doesn't *have to* bother you! It's no big deal. Relax. FOCUS!

At this point you should focus on the skill you are doing, the skill you are about to do, or something else that is immediate, concrete, and constructive. If the distraction happens immediately before your performance, focus your attention on your final preparations for executing your skill; the feel of it, the form of it, the imagery of it, or the strategy of it. For example, take a deep breath, relax as you exhale, imagine the skill or preferred response, then do it.

We do better to focus our energies on things we can control than things we cannot control. We cannot control other people's psychological games, the caliber of competition, or the past preparation of other athletes. We can, however, control our own preparation and our own performance. We can make every effort to do our personal best. No one can ask for more than that; no one can do more than that. Nothing beyond your sincere attempt to do your best really matters. Other competitors are other competitors and you are you, a totally separate entity. If you begin to compare yourself with others, use that as a reminder to focus on your own preparation, your own strategy, your own performance.

Your on-site psych plan and your refocusing plan allow you to enter major events with additional confidence. You have a well thought out and prepracticed plan to make things go right and a plan to use in case something goes wrong. You are ready.

Chapter 16

□

Solving Problems With Coaches

Sometimes the best place to find a helping hand is at the end of your own arm.

Many coaches work extremely hard, have very good intentions, and do a great job, but some are not thinking enough about the athlete and what the athlete needs. They are thinking too much about results or about themselves without giving adequate thought to the athlete as a thinking, feeling human being. Rarely is the athlete consulted enough in the shaping of his or her own destiny.

Common Coaching Errors

A few common coaching errors confront and must be dealt with by most athletes at some time or other. One is some coaches' tendency to become too uptight, "wired," preoccupied, or obsessed with results in the final preparation phase before an important competition. As an athlete, during the last week or two you might feel as though you are being crammed for an exam. At a time when you would gain most from a couple of simple reminders from someone who is supportive, calm, normal, and capable of boosting your confidence, you might be faced with the opposite.

Another common coaching error, which I am happy to say has been on the decline in recent years, is a tendency to constantly try to get you "up" just before an important competition (for example, "This is a crucial game"; "Everything is riding on this"; "All of our work was for this, don't blow it."). If you listen, you can become overactivated; if you don't listen, you may have to cope with a further distraction.

Overload in the final preparation phase, excessive technical input, demands for last-minute changes in familar performance patterns, and an overall excess in felt demands are major reasons why many athletes (and coaches) perform below their potential during important events like the

Olympics and world championships. When an athlete has done a program a hundred times without falling and then screws up his biggest competition of the year, everyone wonders why. The reason is directly related to overload, heightened demands, and the need to perform under a different set of circumstances—mentally. One thing the athlete *doesn't* need at this time is additional stress from his coach.

Another coaching error prevalent at all levels is the failure to give adequate positive, constructive, and supportive feedback. A coach may be quick to tell you that something is wrong yet will not offer specific clues about what to focus on to make things right. While pointing out the things that are wrong she may neglect to comment on the good things or to commend you on your improvement. Likewise, you as an athlete may fail to express appreciation for the good things your coach does. Coaches also need positive feedback and encouragement. They are human too, and most of them really appreciate your constructive comments.

A crucial function of positive feedback is to motivate you, make you feel good about yourself and your efforts, and foster your self-confidence. Statements like "You should be more confident" do nothing to instill additional confidence. But when people's actions and reactions demonstrate their belief in you, your confidence is uplifted. Cutting a person down or harping on the negative undermines self-confidence, whereas a focus on the positive does just the opposite. Hearing about the good things heightens your confidence and makes you feel good about yourself and your effort. Even world champions, who feel fairly confident in their abilities, need positive feedback and appreciate support.

Improving Communication

Learning to give appropriate feedback requires the cooperation of both coach and athlete. Input that is meaningful and well placed is important in training, before competitions, and after performances. Athletes gain nothing from coaches who scold them or totally ignore them after errors or poor performances. They already know, better than anyone else, that they have failed to meet their goal.

How should a coach respond in such situations? The best way to know is to consult with individual athletes. For example, some athletes feel that nothing needs to be said immediately after a loss, but they appreciate support later on. Others prefer physical contact or a word of encouragement, while still others want to know how to avoid similar problems in the future. What works for Jane does not necessarily work for Joe or Jill: Different approaches are needed for different people. Coaches will be more likely to recognize and respond to individual differences (in time to do the maximum good) if athletes help them along through effective communication.

The first step toward improving communication is to recognize that things can be improved; then you have several distinct but interrelated choices:

1. Help your coach to communicate and relate more effectively.
2. Work on improving your own communication.
3. Rely more on yourself to do what is best for you, and fully develop your capacity to direct and control your own behavior.
4. Begin to rely more and more on fellow athletes for support.

It is best if coaches and athletes all work together as distinct components of a finely tuned organism, and share responsibility for directing and improving each of its human parts. A highly respected Chinese badminton coach, Chen Fou Shou, had some interesting comments in this regard:

Wisdom comes from practice: Two heads are better than one. We can make training a success only by listening to the opinions of the players and consulting them whenever we have problems. Some of their suggestions, when adopted, lead to solutions of some urgent problems in training. It is the responsibility of the coach to summarize these suggestions, analyze them, and, in turn, *apply them* in training. . . . Coaches should be good at learning from players and be one with them. Then when shortcomings or difficulties occur in training, the players will sincerely help the coaches to deal with them so that the training will go smoothly.

Sometimes your problems as an athlete are directly related to communication problems with your coach. If you want to get the best out of yourself and your situation, you must be prepared to solve those problems in a mature, responsible way.

The Case of Krista

A promising young gymnast came to see me about quitting. Together we explored her feelings and her options. Within a short time it became clear that her coach was the main source of her anxiety. She said, "My coach puts me down, discourages me, and screams at me."

Recently Krista attempted a maneuver, but something was a little off. The exchange went as follows:

Coach: *That's wrong! Do it again!*

Krista: (attempts the skill)

Coach: *It's still wrong . . . you're not trying!*

Krista: *I'm trying to do it right.*

Coach: *You are not trying. You won't be able to do it. Forget it.*

Krista related to me what happened next. "I then tried to do it again to show her, but everything went wrong. I went home and decided I'd quit. Now I'm not sure what to do." (Her mother had informed me that tears had been flowing regularly at home lately, after practices.) I asked Krista what she had tried to do to improve this situation. "Sometimes I say something back, argue, but it doesn't do any good. The coach just yells more. . . . If the coach is in a really bad mood I just keep my mouth shut, but I'm steaming inside."

I asked, "When the coach does help you perform better or feel better, what does she do?" Krista replied, "She'll be nice to me and tell me, 'You can do it.' She won't scream at me, especially in front of people. She'll smile and help me."

What are Krista's options here?

- She could quit.
- She could find another coach.
- She could try another sport.
- She could hang in there and try to improve her situation.

After we discussed these options, I explained to her that no one can make decisions for other people; they must do that for themselves. What I hoped to do was to help her consider various options. If after exploring some of these options she could not experience sport in a more positive light, then leaving the competition scene might be the best thing for her. Competition in sport, and preparation for it, should not be something to dread.

Krista decided to stay in practice for a week to try out some improvement strategies. Her approach was two-pronged: (a) attempt to exert self-control over her own thinking and her own mood; (b) try to positively influence her coach's behavior.

Self-Control

Krista and I talked about her capacity to control her own thinking and focus, and about who really makes us mad. "Does your coach really make you mad," I asked, "or do you get mad because of the way you respond to the things your coach says? Is it absolutely essential that you get mad when these things are said? Isn't shouting at you or cutting you down a problem or weakness that the coach has, rather than a problem you have? Why should you upset yourself because the coach has a communication problem?"

We talked about possible reasons why the coach would act that way. Krista said, "I guess she's trying to motivate me, to improve me, but it's the opposite with me . . . when she yells at me I get upset and do worse."

My response was, "Even though you may not like what the coach does, it may help if you can interpret the coach's *intent* in a positive way, especially in a potential conflict situation." We also talked a bit about self-support. "One of the problems you sometimes face when trying to correct errors or perfect new moves is that the coach cannot always see minute improvements. It's often viewed as all or none—right or wrong—which of course it really isn't. If your coach doesn't recognize little improvements, or doesn't help you set little goals along the way somewhere between 'wrong' and 'right,' then you have to do it for yourself. You can look for, and feel, small improvements and reinforce yourself or pat yourself on the back for these improvements."

Krista ended up with several refocusing responses that she could think to herself if the coach's shouting became a problem. For example, She's trying to help me improve; I wonder if she could learn to help me improve with a little less volume; There's no need for me to upset myself over her problem; Relax . . . you can control it; What is it that she wants me to try; Focus on doing this move correctly; Smile inside—you are beginning to get things under control.

Influencing the Coach

As athletes, we have to remember that coaches aren't mind readers. You have some responsibility to communicate if you want things to improve. I know that coaches are sometimes not willing to listen. But sometimes they are, particularly if you can find a calm time to talk outside of practice. Consider meeting individually with your coach during a quiet time to talk about your concerns. Tell him what makes you work best or most efficiently, as well as what upsets you and destroys your workout. You might be able to help him improve his effectiveness and help yourself at the same time.

If meeting with the coach seems initially too threatening, then focus on improving on-site communication. Whenever the coach does something that you find helpful, let him know about it right away. For example, when his feedback is good or constructive, thank him. Tell him it helped you. If he has contributed to a good workout or is giving the kind of feedback that you like, communicate this before leaving practice. Help him to help you.

Assist the coach in understanding that you really are trying and do want to improve by asking for additional help or for further clarification on his feedback (for example, "Coach, I'd really like to get this; what specifically should I focus on doing?"). This will help you to get the precise feedback that you want for your skill improvement.

Krista's challenge was to put some of these strategies to work during the upcoming week. I asked her to keep a daily record of how she felt about her skills and her focus in practice so that we would both know how things were progressing.

Krista recorded helpful comments made by her coach as well as her response to them. One of her goals here was to try to catch the coach doing something constructive and to let her know it was appreciated.

What follows is a sketch of Days 1 and 5 of Krista's first week back at practice.

Day 1 Comments.

- I questioned something I didn't understand ("Do you mean this?"). Coach explained.
- I thanked her for the explanation.
- I tried to listen for what she wanted me to do and to look like I was listening.
- I thanked her for the workout.

Day 5 Comments.

- Coach complimented me. I felt great. I thanked her for the compliment and smiled.
- I requested clarification. She responded and showed me how to do it. I thanked her.
- I performed really well.
- Coach joked. I laughed.
- I thanked her for a super workout.

When Krista and I met at the end of the week, it was obvious that her trial week had been a success. About a month later things still seemed to be going well. Krista reported to me, "Coach has been really good lately; she hasn't been getting mad. She doesn't start screaming and yelling for nothing. We talk more, and she even said to come and talk if there's something I'd like to talk about." Communication problems may surface again in the future, but if they do, Krista and her coach should be in a better position to deal with them constructively.

One of the major coaching criticisms relayed to me by experienced national-team athletes is that some of their coaches fail to listen and to act on their input and suggestions. Good coaches will act on your concerns, once you clearly communicate them, because they respect your input and want a good performance result. Others will dig in their heels and resist. Let's hope the resisters will be few.

Even if you meet resistance, you can still take the good things that the coach has to offer. You may also have to prepare yourself to accept, block out, reinterpret, or refocus in the face of the distractions created by the coach. And you can keep working on the coach; miracles sometimes do happen. Your last option, if feasible, is to consider a coaching change that may make you happier and more productive. If you decide to go this route, talk with other athletes who seem to have good relationships with their coaches, try to visit a couple of workouts run by coaches with whom you think you might be compatible, talk with the ones you like, and then make a decision.

Communicate Your Preferences

It is important to communicate your preferences to your coach so that you optimize your chances of performing well in important events. Perceptive coaches who are really interested in helping each athlete perform to capacity will accept and act on the information because it is in everyone's best interest to do so.

Too often, important factors that influence performance are left unmentioned. This is true not only with respect to training sessions but also for competitions. Take, for example, the fact that every single player I interviewed on one professional football team felt that the coach's pregame pep talk, as well as last-minute changes, either were a hindrance or did nothing to contribute to the players' mental preparation for the game. The athletes said, "I'm not motivated by it. I know my job; I'm ready, I don't need him to make me ready." "Rah, rah stuff is of no benefit." As one of the more accomplished players stated, "The standard pregame speech that so many of us have heard before is simply not doing the team or individual players any good. However, it may be a method of tension release for the head coach. Having been in the locker room on many occasions, I think it is. If this is so, he should find another way of doing it, away from the players."

Many athletes in a variety of sports report that their concentration may be broken or their confidence shaken if too many demands are placed on them just before a game. This is not the time for new moves, for new strategies, for changes within routines, for personnel shifts, for altered sequences or combinations, for comments about improving technique, for complicated instructions, or even for requiring athletes to sit and listen. Last-minute changes before competition tend to be more detrimental than helpful in almost every sport, unless athletes have been extremely well trained to adapt to them. For certain athletes they can spell disaster. One thing you don't need is lingering thoughts such as, Maybe . . . I'm not as well prepared as I thought. . . . Maybe the coach doesn't have confidence in me. . . . Maybe the coach doesn't have confidence in the game plan we practiced all week. . . . Maybe I won't be able to perform that well.

As game time approaches, the coach's job of preparing athletes for the contest has been done. He must now shift gears so as not to interfere with the athletes' concentration and last-minute preparations. Some athletes appreciate a word of encouragement, a simple reminder, or a reassuring comment, but most prefer to be left alone during their final mental preparations for the event (for example, "Leave me alone so I can concentrate"; "Watch from a distance so as not to inhibit me"; "I'll call you if I need you."). At high levels in sport, athletes know what they want to do and they have a plan to do it. At all levels in sport it is the athletes' time to perform and the coach's time to free them to do it.

Away from the playing field it is also helpful to talk with your family members, or the people closest to you, about how you can best support one another as you each pursue your goals. Communicate your mutual preferences in a constructive way and without delay, so that each of you becomes aware of how the other is feeling inside and so each has some positive options to consider when attempting to provide mutual encouragement and support.

Helping Your Coach "Cool It"

If your coach (or another person important to you) gets hyper at games or competitions, here are a few ways to help her, as well as yourself. Talk with your coach about her competition behavior. It may help you to know that her "hyperness" is her general way of responding in competitive situations, and not an indication of a lack of confidence in your ability to meet the challenge. Encourage her to develop a precompetition plan, like athletes do, to control her anxiety or at least to reduce it to a manageable level.

Help the coach learn to relax. Suggest a relaxation tape. Reassure her that she has done everything she can do. "You might as well sit back and enjoy it, coach."

Talk with your coach about what you would like her to do, or not do, at the competition site. Be specific in your instructions (for example, "Stay away from me"; "Reassure me"; "Give me a cue word"; "Talk calmly"; "No last-minute changes"; "Give me corrective feedback only at the breakpoint.").

Ask your coach to organize some simulation meets or dress rehearsals. This will give both coach and athlete an opportunity to simulate the desired competition responses (for example, introduction of coach and teams, warm-up, pre-event input, and actual event). Make a commitment to yourself to complete whatever you set out to do, just as you would in a competition. Practice your focus control and make a special effort to overcome any errors or setbacks in a positive way. Have your coach practice appropriate interaction with the athletes (or no interaction), as previously discussed, in the simulated competition. It's also a good opportunity for the coach to practice her relaxation strategies. Give her some feedback on how she did.

If you have an assistant coach or fellow athlete who fits better with your precompetition needs, ask him to interact with you in place of the head coach. I suggested this strategy to some Swedish coaches whose team was preparing for an important tournament. The head coach was very high-strung, whereas the assistant coach was calm and low key. Before the sudden-death elimination match, the two most hyper players on the team interacted only with the calm and reassuring assistant coach. They both played one of the best games of their lives and were instrumental in determining the final outcome, which was in their favor.

Sylvie Bernier also used this approach when winning her gold medal in diving at the Olympic Games in Los Angeles. At Sylvie's request her personal coach, who was great during regular training, sat in the stands during the final practices and the competition, while another coach—who was calmer, more supportive, and less inclined to give last-minute technical input—interacted with her on deck.

Communication is a two-way venture. Both coach and athlete are responsible for making it work. Granted, it is not always easy to communicate your preferences or to discuss your feelings. I have often debated with myself about whether or not I should express certain concerns. However, I'm almost always happy when I do. I simply try to be constructive, tactful, and honest. In some situations it is helpful to offer your coach a relevant book chapter, article, or tape that outlines the benefits of certain approaches, and then follow up with a face-to-face discussion about it. Communication is sometimes a delicate process, but in almost all cases it's worth the effort.

Chapter 17

□

Team Harmony

**In the end, it is upon the quality and commitment
of individuals that all group movements depend.**
Robertson Davies

One of the most satisfying experiences for an athlete or coach is to be a member of a team that gets along well and works as a cohesive unit.

Good communication, respect for one another, a feeling of closeness, a friendly atmosphere, mutual acceptance and encouragement—all make for better workouts, more enjoyable trips, and more satisfying competitions.

Unfortunately, harmony among team members and between coach and athlete is not a trademark of a great number of teams. Sometimes people do not feel appreciated, respected, or accepted and do not get along well together. This can lead to feelings of resentment, interpersonal conflict, performance problems, and withdrawal from the group or the sport.

When sportpsych consultant Cal Botterill studied the moods and performance of Olympic athletes competing at the Moscow Spartakiade, he discovered that team harmony was an important factor influencing performance. Each athlete's mood had a direct effect on his or her performance, and what the athletes cited most often as positively influencing their mood was positive interaction with their coach, roommates, and teammates.

Merely being together in workouts, at competitions, or in social settings like team parties does not necessarily increase mutual liking or harmony among team members. For harmony to develop, people usually must be linked in some interdependent way so that they rely on one another and help one another.

Harmony grows when you really listen to others and when they listen to you, when you are considerate of their feelings and they are considerate of yours, when you accept their differences and they accept yours, when you help them and they help you.

Harmony is grounded in the knowledge that someone really cares about you, appreciates you, respects you, and accepts you as you are. It is when we help others and they help us that we begin to appreciate them. It is when we can get past a person's surface or shell and begin to understand her problems and perspectives in a more intimate way that we feel close to her.

Several national teams with which I have worked have had their fair share of interpersonal conflicts—from members feeling ignored or left out, to athletes feeling that the coach had no respect for them, to people refusing to room with each other, to an actual shoving match on-site before an international event. It is rare that teammates or coaches intentionally create conflict or set out to hurt others' feelings. No one gains from that process, and it usually puts both parties through some unpleasant turmoil that ultimately affects performance. Rather, a lack of awareness of other people's feelings or a misinterpretation of intentions is at the root of many interpersonal problems.

Open communication is an important first step in preventing and solving such problems. It is difficult to be responsive to another's needs or feelings when you do not know what they are. It is difficult to respect another's perspective if you do not understand what it is or where it came from.

The time to communicate is now, at the first sign of confusion or bad vibes. Solve problems when they are small rather than waiting until they have grown out of proportion. This is important both in sport and in other aspects of life.

If you think a coach or teammate is doing something that is affecting the team's performance, talk to that person—directly or through a team representative (for example, the assistant coach, the team captain, or a trusted support staff member). Express both your concerns and your appreciation in an open and genuine manner. Tell people if something they do upsets or pleases you. If you think that something you are doing may be bothering someone, ask that person about it. If you are not sure what someone means, ask for clarification. Help others express what is on their minds.

Resolving Conflicts

When an interpersonal problem exists, even though one party may have been more responsible for creating it, both usually end up sharing the responsibility to implement a workable solution.

There are three ongoing ways to reduce conflict and improve team harmony, which need attention from coaches and athletes alike:

1. *Work on improving your communication skills.* Set a goal to become a better listener, and work on expressing feelings openly and constructively.

2. *Work on improving your skills at helping and receiving help.* Set a goal to give assistance more readily and to receive suggestions more openly and enthusiastically.
3. *Work on improving your own emotional control.* Set a goal to focus and act in a way that lets you and your teammates achieve the best results, and work on refocusing to stay positive or constructive when things don't go your way.

Athletes can often help one another learn, provide challenges for one another, spot for one another, demonstrate for one another, constructively analyze one another's performances, provide a lift or encouragement when needed, and share focus control techniques in a way that benefits all team members. If your teammates know what helps you prepare mentally for your game, they will be in a position to help set the stage for that preparation or at least to avoid inadvertently interfering.

Positive communication and constructive feedback among athletes and between coach and athlete is an extremely important goal in terms of both performance and personal well-being. How many times did that kind of communication happen today? Can you make it happen more often?

The following are additional suggestions offered by athletes for promoting positive interaction:

- Get to know your teammates well.
- Talk with your teammates.
- Listen to your teammates.
- Avoid put-downs.
- Decide that you will get along.
- Take responsibility for yourself, doing what you can to improve the situation.
- Encourage each other.
- Accept individual differences.
- Include everyone.
- Show others that you care.

Harmony is a worthy goal in itself because of the way it makes people feel. But it is important also because it leads to improved performance for all team members.

Making Differences Work for You

There are vast individual differences among members of all teams . . . different personalities, different responses to stress, different coping strategies, different strengths. The differences can work to your advantage and make you stronger as a team *if* you are willing to work together and share your strengths. No coach or athlete knows everything. But when good coaches and good athletes put their heads together, they can know almost everything. One of the veterans may have 10 or 15 years of competitive experience, but as a group you probably have over 200.

My impression is that right now, on many teams, most athletes do things pretty much on their own, keeping many of their good thoughts to themselves. Although there are many individual strengths, there is not much sharing of strengths or feelings.

Your team will be much stronger if you follow these steps:

1. Decide as individuals and as a group that you *really want* to excel.
2. Help one another excel by sharing your strengths. Let me give you some examples: One player can remain incredibly cool in pressure situations, another is superb at analyzing opponents' weaknesses, a third can stay highly motivated in practices to get the most out of them, and a fourth is strong when coming back from behind. How do these athletes make their strengths work? If you can discuss how various team members approach these and other important concerns (for example, focusing for a full game, reacting to errors, supporting teammates, learning from criticism), you can all gain something. No one is totally strong in all areas. We all have room for improvement.

   If a teammate has a problem in some area, you can offer help in a nonthreatening way—saying, for example, "It may not work for you, but I find this works for me." As a team you can review opponents' strategic weaknesses and make tactical suggestions that may be of value to individual players. Regular rap sessions among team members that are open and constructively oriented can do wonders for team morale and overall performance.
3. Encourage one another for trying, and support one another for making any steps in the right direction. At the high performance level, physical skills cease to be enough. Your thoughts and emotions must be working for you. Your task becomes much easier if your teammates and coach are also working for you, or at least not against you.

Building Rapport

What follows is an account of just one of many instances where I've been asked to help resolve conflicts within a team. Coach X calls me with some urgent concerns about interpersonal conflicts on the team. The atmosphere is tension filled, practices are degenerating, spirits are low. Conflicts exist between the coach and certain athletes as well as among some team members. The problem has escalated to the point where practices are being ruined and many people leave practice feeling emotionally upset. The coach is fed up. The athletes are fed up. Coach X describes the situation as desperate.

"Can you help?" is the resounding echo that reverberates through the phone. "I don't know," I say, "but I can come over and give it a try."

How would you go about trying to help? How could your own practice environment be made more positive and productive for both athletes and coaches?

I begin by asking the coach and each athlete a few questions:

- What is the main reason you keep coming to practice?
- If you could change anything you wanted about practice, what would you change?
- Is there anything the coach or other athletes could do to make you feel or work better in the gym? What about at competitions?
- What would make the gym a happier and more productive place to be?
- When the coach is at her best what does she do?
- When the coach is at her worst what does she do?
- What are two things in your life that you like to do best?
- What are your overall goals in your sport?

After reviewing the responses to each question, I speak to the group openly to share their overall views:

Everyone, athletes and coach, says that their involvement in this sport is one of the things in life that they like best. You all want to improve your skills and to have happier, more productive practices. You feel great when you learn a new move or perfect an old one, and so does the coach. Your overall goals are similar, but sometimes you get in each other's way, and as a result nobody achieves their goals. At those times, nobody enjoys being here and nobody learns very much.

The quickest way you can all have happier and more productive practices is by working together and helping one another. What exactly can each of you do to help make that happen? Well, on the basis of your responses to my questions, here are some things your coach can do to make you happier and make you work better in practice. (Listen closely, coach.)

- Encourage you by giving you a reassuring pat on the back or by saying something positive when you make a good effort or improve.

- Give specific directions before you try a new skill and help you understand why things are done in a certain way.
- Tell you what to do if something goes wrong—not yell or ignore you.
- Talk to you, listen to you, show that she likes and respects you.
- Say something positive when you are working well to help keep you working that way; not say that you are "not working hard" or "not trying" when you are.
- Give very specific, helpful corrections—lots of them.
- Smile more, laugh a little, be happy that you are here and show it.

Here are some things you can do to make your coach happier and make your coach work better in practice. (Listen closely, athletes.)

- Say hello and smile when you come in.
- Come to practice with all the personal equipment that you might need.
- Be ready to go when your coach arrives, and work to your maximum during practice.
- Listen closely when your coach gives instructions, look at her, and really try to do what you are asked to do.
- Work well on your own and help each other.
- Remember upcoming events and important dates.
- Remind yourself that your coach is trying to help you reach your goals.
- Tell the coach when you think she has done a good job after practice sessions.

Here's what you can do to make your fellow athletes happier and more productive.

- Say hello, be friendly, and project a good mood when you come in.
- Encourage teammates. For example, compliment them if they are doing well and help cheer them up if they are having difficulties (for example, "It's OK—you'll get it next time.").
- Work to correct difficulties instead of complaining or getting upset if something is off; ask others for tips to improve.
- Help each other with everyday tasks. For example, take out, move, or adjust equipment together; spot for each other; or run drills with a partner.
- Help each other to improve skills. For example, if you know how to do something or you see a mistake being made, feel free to give tips to any teammate who is willing to accept help. Point out what is good and what needs work.

Obviously, a coach cannot give individualized feedback to all athletes at the same time, particularly in sports where there are many players or several events going on at once. However, teammates can watch, correct, advise, and encourage each other. Fellow athletes can often see and understand, better than anyone, what you are doing or not doing.

In an attempt to dramatize the interdependence of people in a team setting, I invite Coach X's group to play a little game. The name of the game is "Ping," and the rules are quite simple. "For the next 5 minutes during practice, if anyone says anything or does anything that makes you feel good, you say 'ping.' Let's say that Jane just told me, 'Thanks for trying to help us make our practices better.' That makes me feel good, so I say, out loud, 'Terry pings Jane.'

"OK, let's try it." Practice commences. After 5 minutes no pings have ponged upon my eardrums. Yet a few pingable things have been done. We rehuddle the team.

"Jane, you say that when coach gives specific instructions and then points out what is good, you feel happy. She just did that on your mount. That's a ping.

"Coach, you say that when an athlete is ready to go, that makes you happy. When you walked to the bars Jane was ready and raring to go—that's a ping.

"Let's try it again, this time looking for the positive things, the pings."

It starts slowly, but before long the gym is popping with pings. It is contagious. An athlete does a good jump, the coach smiles and says, "Good" . . . ping. The athlete smiles and says, "Thanks" . . . ping. The coach feels good for the thanks . . . ping.

I watch two athletes working out side by side on two balance beams in the far corner of the gym. One says to the other, "That was nice." She gets a ping, and pings in return. Her teammate then watches her try a move. "That's better than it was!" She gets pinged. "You can do that"—ping. "Good!"—ping. Coach pings Sue; Sue looks back over her shoulder, smiles at the coach and sings out, "I got a ping." The coach smiles in return—ping.

As an introduction to group support, "Ping" works well with these young athletes. I'm not sure whether it would work with all groups, but the game's playfulness serves to loosen things up and also brings to life an important message. The "pinging" *concept* is applicable to all groups.

To help keep things rolling on a positive note, I integrate some of the "happy workout suggestions" onto index cards. The cards are distributed to the athletes and the coach as helpful reminders, or cue cards, for subsequent practices. The goal is to do as many of the actions listed on one card as possible in one practice session, and to do the remaining ones at the next practice.

Sample Cue Cards

Coach Reminders—I

1. Absolutely no yelling—no matter what happens, stay cool.
2. Smile—show you are in a good mood.
3. Point out what is good, then correct constructively.
4. After giving correction, briefly explain why.
5. Say something positive not related to the sport.

Coach Reminders—II

1. Give positive feedback every chance you get.
2. Laugh a little—loosen up.
3. Give specific instruction and encouragement.
4. Tell the athletes what they did well tonight.
5. Say goodnight and leave the gym happy.

Coach Reminders—III

1. Show that you care and want each athlete there.
2. Say hello to everyone sometime today.
3. Give everyone some individual feedback sometime today.
4. Listen closely when athletes give input or express a feeling.
5. Respect and act upon the athletes' input.
6. Feel good about your own progress.

Athlete Reminders—I

1. Smile and say hello to everybody.
2. Stop, look (eye contact), and listen when the coach is correcting you. Make a real effort to correct the skill.
3. Be ready to go—stand tall.
4. Help a teammate tonight.
5. If your coach or another athlete has been helpful, tell her that you appreciate it.

Athlete Reminders—II

1. Think happy tonight—make someone else feel happy too.
2. Ask the coach what you should do to make something better, then really try.
3. Give 100% focus and effort on your routines today.
4. Watch a teammate and compliment her on something she does well.
5. If anyone is getting discouraged, try to cheer her up.
6. Tell the coach that she really helps you learn when she encourages you.

Follow-Up

To find out how practices were affected by this attempt to improve team harmony, one of my sportpsych students observed Coach X's team for 2 weeks before and 2 weeks after the intervention. The rate of positive verbal interaction (for example, praise, compliments, and encouragement) doubled; the rate of physical assistance in learning doubled; and, most importantly, negative criticism (for example, yelling and put-downs) was almost completely eliminated.

The coach commented, "Everything is working out much better now. Everyone seems to be more happy and relaxed. All the girls seem to be really working and trying hard. We can even get through a couple of practices in a row now without any tears or pouting." Will she do anything differently as a result? She says that she will "use more positive reinforcement and treat the girls more individually."

I hope she does, because it makes an incredible difference. Coach X will have to be persistent because it is easy to fall into old patterns. She will gain from the athletes' assistance.

The moral of this story is that everyone on a team, even in individual sports, is linked like a family. What you do, and how you respond to others, has an effect on how others feel and how they respond to you. To make this kind of family happy and productive, each of you has to do your part. It may take a little extra effort in the beginning, but it's worth it in the end. When you encourage each other, help each other, listen to each other, correct each other in a positive way, and support each other, everybody will be happier, work harder, and learn more. We will all leave the team as better people.

Chapter 18

□

Losing as a Learning Experience

**A refined ability to learn from failure and to grow through losses
is necessary to achieve excellence in any human endeavor.**

Losing in Sport

I remember my first experience at the U.S. Eastern Intercollegiate Gymnastics Championships particularly well. It was my second year at Syracuse University, where I had accepted a gymnastic scholarship after having won almost everything I entered as a youngster and a teenager. I had worked especially hard during the summer and the regular season to regain lost ground that resulted from an injury sustained during my first year of university competition. The injury had sidelined me for the season. I guess I wanted to prove something to myself and those around me, and I also wanted to feel worthy of my scholarship. A good deal of my effort had been concentrated on the trampoline, as this was the first event I could get back to after my injury. During the season I consistently outscored my competitors and felt that I had a really good shot at winning the title. Actually, I thought I would win it, and so did most of my teammates. I had prepared well and was ready—so I thought. I remember hearing my name called, jumping up on the tramp, bouncing high into the air, throwing one trick, and landing on the springs. That was the end of my routine—the end of my hopes—the end of my dreams. At that time, if you touched the springs your routine was terminated.

What a way to end the season! I was really quite depressed. All I wanted to do was to get out of there, which I did. I didn't want to hear anyone's "Oh, it's OK" comments; I didn't want to talk to anyone; I didn't want to eat; and I wasn't looking forward to responding to the standard questions like "Did you win?" or "What happened?" when I returned to campus. I was down for about 2 weeks. It doesn't seem very important now, but at the time it was probably the most important thing in my world.

Significant losses have a way of colliding with our self-esteem. The vibrations can result in self-doubt, self-damnation, worry, and even guilt feelings. Though these thoughts can become overwhelming, there is no reason they have to be. It's helpful to remember that this loss is not you—it is something that you are currently experiencing. You are so many more things to yourself and to others than this loss. You can deal with the experience of loss and grow from it. The hurtful feelings will fade—they always do. Even though you have lost, you have gained something from the experience, and you are a stronger person—perhaps even a better competitor—for it.

Now what did I accomplish by coming down on myself, by denying myself enjoyment, by punishing myself? I had in fact failed to meet an important goal that I felt had been a realistic one. I had in fact carried out one of the worst performances of my career when it was most important for me to do my best. However, I hadn't *tried* to do poorly. The fact that I was trying so hard probably contributed to my problem in the first place. I was overactivated—too pumped up. As a result I threw the first trick so hard that I overrotated and headed for the springs. Was this a just reason to be mad at myself?

That particular loss turned out to be a golden opportunity to learn something that is difficult to learn under any other circumstances. Instead of telling myself how I had blown it, how lousy I was, how I had let people down, how I'd wasted the year, how I'd let all those hours go down the drain, and so on, I began to approach the situation from an entirely different angle. OK, I thought, so I failed to accomplish an important goal. I'm disappointed, but it's not the end of the world. It doesn't mean that I'm a no-good, worthless person. It has nothing to do with my overall human value. It has to do with my ability to perform a certain kind of skill, under specific conditions, in a certain frame of mind.

What can I learn from the experience that may help me perform better under similar conditions in the future, if I choose to do so? Well, maybe I can learn that I have to be a little less activated in championship competitions, and maybe I should begin to experiment with strategies to accomplish this. Perhaps I should wait until the bounce is centered and feels right before starting the first trick.

I do know that it does me no good to upset myself, nor does it help my teammates, my friends, my family, or my performance. No matter how hard I try, I cannot control the past; that I must accept. I can only work in the present and for the future.

I finally did begin to get my head together. I began to look for positive lessons from an unfortunate experience. I asked myself, What did I learn about myself? What did I learn about those around me? What did I learn that can help me in the future? Only then did losing become a positive learning experience. I think that largely because of that learning, I was able to go back the following year and win the Eastern Intercollegiate title and the NCAA Regional title as well. From that time on, the perspective that I took into sport allowed me to gain something from the experience itself, regardless of numerical outcomes or the achievement of preset goals.

Even the greatest performers fail, but many of them have developed strategies to help them learn or benefit from these experiences. They don't like falling short of a goal, but they do not view it as a personal disaster or an indication of personal inadequacy. They merely conclude that this time this particular approach didn't work, or their focus wasn't fully enough absorbed in the task. They don't tear themselves down in response to loss, they simply prepare better or differently for the next opportunity, which may be in or outside of a sporting context.

To lose is to be human . . . and we are all human (well, most of us are, anyway). Every thinking, feeling, living person experiences loss. No one escapes it—not even the greatest of the greats. "Your task is to make the journey from immediate loss to eventual gain as rapidly, smoothly and comfortably as possible" (Colgrove, 1976, p. 22).

We tend to be most susceptible to feeling down when we expect to do well and do poorly instead, when we expect to win and we lose, when we expect love or acceptance and experience rejection. In such cases, sometimes our expectations have been unrealistic; sometimes we have not prepared or focused as well as we could have, and we can work on this; and sometimes we have done everything in our power to make things happen (given the constraints of our time and resources) and, for reasons totally beyond our control, events do not go as we hoped or planned. It is important to recognize the difference between matters that are within our control and those that are beyond it. "Fight for the highest attainable aim but never put up resistance in vain" (Selye, 1956, p. 300).

As sport psychologist Robert Nideffer (1976) pointed out, if we become wrapped up in our loss or our depression, we fail to effectively use the energy that we do have. Instead of directing our limited energy toward positive ends we direct it toward negative ends, to the betterment of no one.

Loss can make you feel miserable, distressed, and helpless. But it can also challenge you to test your strength, draw on your capacity to cope, get to know yourself better, examine your priorities, and reflect on *where* you are going, *why*, and *how*. A time of loss can broaden your perspective and redirect your course, in sport or in life. As unpleasant as it may be, loss can result in your learning how to better prepare for, influence, avoid, or cope with situations that may arise in the future. If you can draw anything good out of your loss, or put what remains in perspective, loss is no longer totally hopeless.

The route to personal excellence and self-realization is full of ups and downs, progressions and regressions, great leaps forward, backslides, and plateaus. But as long as the overall direction is up, you will ascend the mountain—and there are *many* mountains in this life, all of different textures.

Life is a constant process of adaptation; the better you can cope, the happier, healthier, and more fulfilled you will be. If you can view difficulties and setbacks as a challenge, as a test of your inner strength, as an opportunity for personal growth, then you can turn these experiences into victory. Attempting to learn from less than ideal circumstances has an interesting way of putting you back in control.

Losing at Love

All of us experience loss, whether it means failure to meet a goal, defeat in a competition, the breakup of a relationship, or the death of a loved one. The degree to which loss affects us, and our means of coping with it are very individual, regardless of what we lose. Once you explore some constructive approaches for handling personal loss, you will likely have ample opportunity to apply them both in and out of sport.

Losing at love often occurs when two people grow in different directions, when they no longer meet each other's needs, when expectations are unrealistic, or when one partner finds someone else who better meets his or her needs.

Such loss has the potential to be devastating, but it can also lead to significant personal growth. When a relationship breaks up, often your first inclination is to see yourself as an overall failure. But the parting of a relationship does not imply that either person is a failure as a human being. It is often merely the fact that people change—their wants, needs, perspectives, and desires change. Nothing is static in this world, people least of all. The way in which individuals view themselves, each other, and the world is in a constant state of flux. What began as a good fit can become a misfit for at least one partner. Sometimes people may be incompatible to begin with, but it may take time for them to realize it. You may still be the world's best peach, but your partner may be more compatible with a banana or a lemon. Once you recognize this you can begin to move forward in constructive and positive ways without upsetting yourself to no avail.

The thoughts that first fill our heads, following a loss at love, are often not based on fact. They are an illusion; the reality lies in recognizing the illusion for what it is. Sometimes it is hard to avoid self-destructive thoughts, particularly when losses are unexpected (and they usually are). But it is important to straighten out your thoughts as soon as possible and to recognize that your loss isn't the end of the world. You really do have a lot of good qualities. This is a time to focus on your strengths, not to keep searching for weaknesses or flaws. We all have weaknesses. But we also have strengths that we can appreciate, that certain other people can appreciate, and that many can gain from.

There *is* life after loss. Much lies ahead in terms of meaningful pursuits and quality people. Sometimes our losses actually open up new opportunities that enrich our lives in ways that would otherwise not have been possible. A loss at love can lead to personal growth if we accept what was good in the relationship and take the time to honestly and constructively draw out lessons on how we can improve ourselves and our future relationships. The mending of broken hearts rests with the regained belief in ourselves and our future.

If you are ever feeling terribly depressed, remember that despair lifts over time. Depressed moods and helpless feelings don't last forever. Time heals all but the most mortal wounds, and using your time positively speeds up your own healing process. Your vision is often clouded or shortsighted when you are down; there is almost always something meaningful, a reason for living, just around the corner.

A few years after the breakup of a relationship that had caused me much emotional turmoil, it no longer seemed so vitally important. A decade later it had very little significance, outside of some important memories and the important lessons that I learned and could carry into future relationships. What will these losses mean when I look back in 20 years, 100 years, 1,000 years?

I can look back objectively because I realize that what I thought was the end of the game was really only the beginning. Perhaps it was the end of an inning, but there were many more innings that told a different story, and there are still many more to come.

Chapter 19

□

Crawling Out of the Helplessness Hole

Grant me serenity to accept the things I cannot change; the courage to change the things I can; and the wisdom to know the difference.
Reinhold Neibuhr

One major obstacle to living out our potential has been referred to as "learned helplessness." It was first demonstrated in experiments with animals (Seligman, 1975). A dog was put in a cage and given an electrical shock through the floor of the cage. The dog could not escape the shock even by running frantically to the other side. A small barrier was then placed across the center of the cage, and the dog was shocked again. This time all the dog had to do was to step over the barrier, and he could escape the shock. What do you think he did? He lay down, whimpered, and accepted the shock. Once the dog had "learned" that he could not escape the shock he didn't even try to escape it, even though he now could. That's an example of learned helplessness.

This also happens with human beings. The real world shocks people a few times, and they come to believe that they have no control over the situation or over themselves. Once this learning occurs they tend to stop trying because of the belief that trying has no effect. Yet in many cases, people are fully capable of stepping over the barrier and effecting positive change. It is the belief that their responses are futile that produces their state of helplessness, even though the belief may be totally inaccurate.

If, through a series of setbacks, you come to believe that your situation is hopeless, that you are helpless and have absolutely no control, your view can become distorted and self-defeating. Even when events are within your potential control, you may not see it or believe it.

People often consider themselves less effective, talented, and valued than they really are, especially when feeling down. During down times, small obstacles are perceived as impossible barriers; simple setbacks or even moderate improvements are viewed as evidence of complete failure.

Many events that you see as outside your control are actually within your control if you are willing to act and to be persistent in your actions. Learned helplessness is your only barrier to personal control.

To escape from the learned helplessness hole, you must first begin to recognize and accept that it is possible to effect change in your own thinking and in events in your own life. The only way the experimenters could get the "helpless" dogs to recognize that they were not helpless was to actually drag them across the cage to the side where there was no shock. We humans are supposed to be a lot smarter than dogs, but sometimes when we feel helpless or depressed we must also drag ourselves, or be dragged, into action. Sometimes we can simply decide that it is possible to do something and do it. At other times, it helps if a friend provides some encouragement, gives us a gentle nudge or a push, or drags us out—to the other side of the cage. Sometimes simple reassurance from a respected source that you can exercise control over yourself or your situation is enough to get you going. Once you recognize that you can change or control things if you so choose, you are essentially out of the hole. There are, of course, certain things beyond your control. For example, you cannot control the past, and you must accept it as a given. You can, however, control your own thoughts about the past, as well as many events that lie in the future.

When trying to cope with depressing thoughts or to regain control, it is critical that you somehow *confirm* your control over some aspect of your life. Taking control of seemingly small elements of life can have an incredibly uplifting effect, particularly when you are feeling a lack of control. So if you find yourself in a hole and want to climb out, decide to do something and then do it! The fact that you have exercised your capacity to decide, and then to act, is satisfying in itself and lifts you.

Certain things can make each of us feel better when we are momentarily overcome by feelings of helplessness. For me it may be having a long run, spending time with a loved one (child or adult), eating a good meal, canoeing, hiking along a trail in the woods, cross-country skiing, writing, relaxing in a jacuzzi, listening to music, or sitting in front of a fire. For others it might be taking a long, hot bath or shower, snacking on chocolate chip cookies and cold milk, doing crafts, picking berries, gardening, building something, reading a good book, buying something they have put off buying, making or eating ice cream, or seeing a good movie. These may sound like simple things, but they start with self-directed decisions that lead to enjoyable action or interaction, and they give you an important sense of control over at least some part of your destiny. I have found that something as simple as deciding to go for a run, and then going, can provide a sense of control and exhilaration that makes my day.

If you start feeling helpless, do something that you enjoy in an area totally unrelated to the one that created the helpless feeling. It helps initially if you choose something at which you know you can succeed—run a short distance, make spaghetti, build something, whatever—but be persistent. Don't give up halfway through or you might feel worse. You are trying to demonstrate to yourself that you can choose to do something and then do it, that you can exercise control of some aspect of your life.

Before I learned to lift myself, if I began to feel helpless I tended to deny myself the very things that might have helped overcome this feeling. For example, I wouldn't take the time to run, or build a fire, or make a good meal, or share time with someone I cared about. But I discovered that indulging in those simple pleasures could lift me and make me feel much better. The process of doing something simple like preparing food can divert my attention and give me a sense of control—and I end up enjoying a good meal (well—sometimes it isn't that great, but I still enjoy eating it).

Now I try to use a helpless feeling as a signal to do something that I really enjoy. I can assure you that it's a much better strategy than sulking or feeling sorry for yourself. If you deprive yourself of the things you like, you merely add another burden to the one you are already carrying.

As Thoreau astutely pointed out, "Birds never sing in caves." You must have the courage to spread your wings to get out of the cave, which is at least partially of your own making. Lift yourself, support yourself, and look for the rays of sunshine. Only then will you want to sing and be sung to.

If you are feeling really down, it takes time to get in touch with your feelings, to get your head together, and to separate illusion from reality. Sitting quietly beside a calm lake or walking through a beautiful scenic area provides an excellent opportunity to begin to clear your thoughts. You can't rush this process. Take your time. Feel down if you feel like feeling down. Just don't be down for too long.

As you are regaining your strength, it might give you an additional lift to help someone else or to receive help from someone. It is also an ideal time to engage in some diversion. By directing your attention to other activities you give yourself temporary relief and make yourself feel better. This lets you return to your situation with renewed energy or with a refreshed outlook. If you want total diversion, pick something that really absorbs your focus. For me, watching a really gripping film, playing with a group of 5-year-olds, snuggling with the right person, or canoeing on white water can do just that. When you start down a set of rapids you are obliged to focus your attention on reading the water in order to choose a suitable course through the many obstacles. The price for not paying attention is high: a total wipeout. When your attention is focused in this manner, you cannot at the same time be thinking about your disappointment at losing.

It is true that diversion is only a temporary solution, because you must eventually deal with your belief about the loss and about your own capacities. However, it gives you a break and can help you recognize that you are valued and valuable in yourself. Once you realize this, you are no longer helpless. The sun begins to shine because you accept yourself in victory and in defeat as an equally worthy person.

Chapter 20

□

Overload and Adaptation for Life

To the "more" of life—the real revolution.
Trina Paulus

Overload. Every time it happens, I know it. I feel myself being pulled in too many directions at once. I start moving faster physically, and my guts tie up in a knot as I try to meet everyone's demands, including my own. I become more irritable toward other people, especially those I love, not because they are necessarily the ones making the demands but because they just happen to be around. Once I settle down and become more relaxed, I reflect; I don't like being in that overload state and think that it was ridiculous to get caught up in it. So I decide that I am not going to let that happen again.

I try to prevent overload by staggering meetings, commitments, and other scheduled activities so that they are not back to back, with one still incomplete while another is starting. If I see an overload coming on I remind myself, Take a few minutes to relax—it won't do you any good to get yourself upset over this; you can only do so much. That reminder in itself can put me in a healthier frame of mind.

From time to time, I still find myself being overwhelmed by external demands or by self-induced pressure. Most of the time, though, I can predict how much I can handle comfortably and adjust my pace before getting into trouble. This often means saying no to people, situations, or requests, but it means saying yes to life. We have to remind ourselves continually that we must direct the course of our own lives, rather than let others direct our lives for us.

As you begin to gain profile as an athlete, an entertainer, or a person skilled in any field, more demands are placed on you. The higher the profile, the more the demands. Following the Olympic Games, for example, medalists face all kinds of additional demands. Everyone wants a piece of you, and if you give them all what they want, there will be nothing left for you or for your loved ones. There are too many requests—from agents, media people, and the public; for interviews, appearances, responses to fan mail, and so on—and not enough time or energy in any one life to fulfill them.

If you find yourself in that situation, *you* must take control. Decide how much you can realistically handle and how much you want to take on. Maybe you feel you can handle two outside appearances, media interviews, or talks a month, but none during training camps or before important competitions. You will probably find that you cannot answer all your letters and calls, so you can either get someone to help you carry that load or not answer them. It is crucial to set priorities and follow them. Otherwise you can be sucked dry by people who really don't know or care about you as a person and who don't realize how difficult it is just to keep up your commitments to training and to loved ones, let alone to meet outside requests.

A little overload, or even a lot, every now and then won't kill you, but a continuous diet of overload and stress can destroy you: your health, your performance, and your happiness.

As high-performance athletes take on additional outside demands, they often find that they are no longer respecting the patterns that allowed them to reach the top. Even if they continue to train as hard, the extra demands sap their energy and compromise important rest time.

Most people never come close to gaining the profile of an Olympic champion, but all of us face times when the demands of life seem greater than our capacity to meet them. To avoid overload, you must first think about priorities. What are your priorities at this point in life? List them! Next, determine how many things you can do well at the same time. How many commitments can you take on and still pursue your priorities? Set some guidelines to ensure that you schedule enough time for quality rest, quality preparation, and enjoyment in living. Then follow those guidelines!

The first line of defense against a highly stressful lifestyle is a plan to prevent overload. Focus on maintaining a desirable pace of life, and adjust as soon as the pace becomes uncomfortable. The second line of defense is to learn to relax in the face of stress and between the stresses you face. Worrying about deadlines, about being late or not ready for something, or about meeting multiple commitments creates stress. Predicting and pre-planning can solve many problems related to such demands. Be realistic in making commitments; that is, overestimate rather than underestimate the amount of time, energy, and work involved in getting something done. Start preparing earlier to meet deadlines. Leave early enough to arrive on time without having to rush. Accept the fact that at certain times you will have to stop working on one thing to start on another.

Spread out your commitments over a reasonable schedule and leave more time between them. Accepting a series of commitments for a time that seems far in the future can come to haunt you in the present. Set priorities so that you say yes only to things you really want to do and no to the rest.

Before saying yes to anything that makes additional demands on your limited time, try to find out exactly what the cost will be in time and energy. It always takes more time than they tell you. A "10-minute" interview often ends up taking a couple of hours out of your life—talking on the phone, making arrangements, thinking about what to say, getting there, waiting until they are set up and ready for you, getting home, and so on. In agreeing to a request indicate exactly how much time and commitment you are willing, and not willing, to give. Set your conditions and call the shots *before* you accept.

If you are not sure whether you want to do it, my advice is simple: Don't! Your life is not going to suffer, or be any less fulfilling, for not doing it. It will probably be better, because you will have a little more time for you. I once saw a button that read, "Enjoy life—this is not a dress rehearsal." Good advice. So if you are not sure whether this additional demand will help you enjoy your life more, at least delay committing yourself. Give yourself a few days to assess the urgency of the request to see how it fits with your overall schedule and priorities.

Remember the word *no*. It is sometimes hard to say, but it is often the only way to maintain a high level of performance and preserve a balanced and healthy lifestyle. I have found that being honest with *no*s, and sometimes asking the advice of the person making the request, reduces my level of stress (for example, "I would like to do it, but I have so many commitments already that I simply can't fit it in and still maintain any quality in my life. . . . What would you do in my situation?").

If I am going to say yes more often, it should be to things that are personally satisfying (for example, time with special people, time for things I really enjoy or find relaxing). It's not a question of working any less diligently while you are training, it is a question of easing your outside commitments and relaxing more outside of training or working hours.

Let's say that you are already overcommitted and under stress. It is a bit difficult (though not impossible) to replan a schedule that was set some time ago or to rearrange existing commitments. For the moment, though, you can avoid additional stressors (for example, further requests, new demands, telephone calls, interruptions). Seek out a quiet place where you won't have to answer your phone or your mail. Allow yourself a little time to relax and regenerate, in order to meet your current demands as best you can.

Even if multiple commitments make you late for a deadline, don't blow it out of proportion. This time you will be late. It is not going to kill you or them. Relax. Slow down. Learn something from the incident about controlling your own schedule to prevent it from repeating itself. The world won't end if you miss this deadline. It is not worth getting stressed out. Relax. Take a walk. Enjoy a few minutes of your life.

Listen—slow down and *relax—*you know when you're getting over-loaded. Physical signs, mental signs, and changes in feelings tell you. You may start to feel tense, grumpy, irritated by things that normally do not bother you, or you may begin to feel drained, uncomfortable, or out of control. Your body is telling you to slow down, but you are not listening. If you begin to heed your personal signs and relax your pace before the overload, you can save yourself a lot of grief. Don't rush everywhere and through everything. Take it easy. Move in an unhurried fashion. When you sit down to talk with someone, relax, listen, and then relax again for a few moments before responding. Slow down when you walk or drive from one event to another. Walk relaxed. Run relaxed. If the phone rings, relax for a few rings before responding, or if you would prefer to avoid additional demands, don't answer it at all. Relax in the shower, in front of a fire, in the sauna. Eat relaxed and drink more slowly. After eating, take a little time to do nothing but enjoy some quiet time alone or with loved ones. Relax a bit every day by listening to music; getting yourself into a soothing, relaxing environment; relaxing the muscles in your body; stretching out on the grass; or doing whatever makes you feel good. Try to relax more in stressful settings. If necessary, take a 5-minute time-out from the stress-related event, to relax or be alone with your thoughts.

If people you love are suffering or feeling neglected because of your overload, communicate with them about your feelings. Let them know that what is really upsetting you is your overload, and that they are not the cause of your short temper, anger, or unhappiness. Let them know that you are trying to get it under control. They will appreciate knowing that your behavior has been your way of responding to the pressure, and they can often help you to cope in more constructive ways. For example, when they see that you are becoming upset, they might give you an agreed-upon reminder such as "Relax, it won't do any good to upset yourself, lighten up, take a break"; "It's time to put that refocusing stuff to work." Sometimes your own reminders—a note on your wall or even a happy face drawn on your little finger—can help. The long-range challenge is to prevent overload; to live more fully, feeling the way you like to feel; and to experience more of life. Put to song by the music group, the Temptations, the goal is: "To live the life you love and love the life you live."

Chapter 21

□

From Hero to Zero

The challenge is not only to pursue excellence but to do so without destroying the rest of your life.

A bronze medal winner in the summer Olympic Games had a coach who had convinced her that excelling in swimming was the only really important thing in her life. He persuaded her that all those other people out there (outside the pool regimen) were "vegetables" because they "weren't doing anything." As she expressed it, "Then I stopped swimming and became one of them." It took her many years to regain confidence in herself as a person.

People can set unrealistic and untrue expectations for you that can ultimately hurt you. If someone leads you to believe that you are vitally important only because you are ranked second or third in the world, then what is left for you when you are no longer ranked? To become a vegetable?

I'm concerned about the all-consuming marriage to sport (or work). I'm concerned about the breakup of this marriage, especially when the human being is tossed out feeling, I'm no longer good enough to be here; without this I'm nothing. That is a difficult feeling for anyone to cope with. The person facing this situation may retire feeling, "The sport lives on and I die a quiet death without too many people seeming to care. I am an artist. I paint with my body. I cannot separate my own value from my art. Yet my art is for the moment and vanishes in a flash—and I can no longer paint. So what value have I?"

Growing apart from one's sport certainly doesn't have to produce these feelings, but it does far more often than I would like.

All dedicated athletes have a common commitment to fulfill a dream of excellence. But is it necessary to shut out the rest of your life? For most world-class athletes, sport is the main focus in life, particularly during their years of greatest improvement. However, it is important to distinguish between "the most important thing" and "the only thing" in life. Both allow you to pursue excellence, but only one allows you to do so without sacrificing the rest of your life.

Something has to suffer when one phase of your life, such as sport or work, weighs too heavily for too long a time. It may be your personal growth, your family life, your health, your sanity—or something else. When you no longer have time to be playful or no longer know how to play, when the smile is gone from your life, something is out of balance.

It is possible to pursue high levels of excellence without destroying the rest of your life, but only if some balance is built into your ongoing program. *Balance* implies that there is time for developing the playful side of life and time for relaxed intimacy with others; that athletes are treated as worthy and loved humans, apart from their performances; and that someone really cares when athletes are in the process of adapting to other meaningful pursuits. I am suggesting a balanced form of excellence that respects the other phases of life. This balance allows you to win more from life in the long run.

The Decision to Retire

The athletes who emerge the best adjusted in the years following their retirement from a sport are those who were able to balance their lives during their competitive years. No doubt, sport received their highest commitment for a good portion of their competitive lives, but other pursuits were not relegated to a value of zero. Important people and pursuits remained alive and important, while necessarily receiving less attention during the period of highest commitment. The trick in achieving balanced excellence in life is to establish priorities for different times and spaces, and to let each move into and out of prominence as you see fit.

No matter how important sporting excellence may be, it is a short-term venture. The average life expectancy of competitors at the highest performance level is about 6 years. It is a hard climb up and a fast slide down. An athlete's career can terminate, or be terminated, very suddenly for a variety of reasons. All athletes, including Olympic champions and professional superstars, are destined to become has-beens. Sporting glory is short-lived.

To shed some light on the retirement process as experienced by elite athletes, Brigitte Bitner and I conducted an investigation. One of Brigitte's many strengths is that she was an Olympian in high jumping. She was contemplating her own retirement from competition at the time of our study.

Seventy-nine former Olympic athletes (males and females) representing 11 sports responded to a series of questions about their retirement experiences. Upon reflecting on their overall athletic career, 96 percent of this group felt that their involvement in sport had been a generally positive experience. Retirement was a different story. Sixty-one percent reported feelings of panic or fear when faced with the final decision of leaving high performance sport.

A former two-time Olympian expressed it this way:

Intensive training is a lifestyle that can lead to both psychological and physical addiction. Cutting this out of your life can leave you feeling void of any resources to fulfill basic needs (for example, tension release, goal attainment, achievement, or personal satisfaction). Somehow our elite sporting society must be changed so that the worth of the individual is based on more than skill alone, so that when skill is gone or reduced, you are not less than a person. Athletes should be channeling some of their strengths into something other than just training and competition. But this needs to begin prior to retirement, before athletes are turned off or burned out. This process can start at the beginning of their training.

To quote another athlete who had an exceptionally difficult transition:

At the age of 16 I had a nervous breakdown and spent the following 2 years in and out of mental hospitals. . . . My sport and competing was my life. One evening I had had enough and decided that the sport circus was not worth my efforts any longer. In the beginning I felt like a failure because I thought that I had given up before reaching my peak. My father, who is very ambitious, did not like to see me quit, especially because of my potential to succeed. It took me a long time to accept myself after retiring. I couldn't see daily success in everyday life. I put on weight and neglected staying in shape. . . . It is difficult to retire because high-level competition in sport is a way of life; one has to give up everything in order to compete and travel with the team. The large step back into normal life is difficult (lack of education, no profession, no intimate relationships). On the positive side, I was a person again, not just an athlete. I had a chance to go back to school, I had more time for friends and meaningful relationships. I underwent a change in values, got out of the rat race of having to be successful in order to be happy.

Based on my personal experience, what I would suggest to make retirement easier for others is to make it possible for the athlete to lead a more normal life (for example, less traveling, better education, more active social life and home life, cultural activities). Then the change would not be so traumatic.

Although for some athletes the retirement experience was very difficult, others had a relatively easy transition out of high-level competition. One athlete said, "I thought it was easy. I had other hobbies, a career, and a personal life that could easily be expanded and improved." Athletes who have relatively stress-free retirement experiences seem to have one or more of the following things going for them: They have been preparing for retirement during their competitive years; they have meaningful options to slot into upon retirement; and they have the complete support of at least one important person upon retirement or immediately afterward (for example, a parent, coach, close friend, or loved one).

Following are some of the major suggestions from the athletes in the study. Before the retirement decision:

- Find a coach who deals with the whole athlete rather than just the competition part. A more personal approach can help you leave with a feeling of being worthwhile after many years of dedicated training.
- Consider your personal development as it relates to school, work, family, and friends an integral part of your overall training program.
- Take a little more time to relax and enjoy something else.
- Take some time to assess what you want from competition and from yourself. Get to know yourself well enough to decide what is best for you.
- Have at least a strong idea of a new career and begin to prepare for it before retirement.
- Try to learn some skills in other sports that you can engage in all your life (for example, skiing, fishing, golfing, canoeing).
- Change your routine in the off-seasons. Go to college or do something else.
- Make time for things other than training and competition. Incorporate or actually schedule other activities into your overall program (for example, leisure activities, social activities, educational activities). Include them in more than a token manner.
- Use your sport expertise and experience. Let younger athletes gain from your knowledge and experience, talk to youth groups, conduct or assist at clinics for coaches and athletes, take coaching certification courses, coach, teach, get involved with sports governing bodies, develop programs, and the like. Focus some of your energy in areas where you are already accomplished. Try your hand at this while still actively competing so that if it interests you, the option is there for continuation or expansion after retirement.
- Think of retirement as an opportunity to learn something new, to grow, to develop in other areas.

After the retirement decision:

- Once your decision has been made, let your coach, family, and friends know that it would be really great to have their support.

- Consider academic pursuits, job training, business opportunities, commercial ventures, and the like in an area where you already have strengths or in any other area that really interests you.
- Stay actively involved in sports or fitness activities. Continue working out at a fun level, participate in self-paced activities, or get involved in "veterans" events. Adjust your goals accordingly.
- If possible arrange for a sharing of experiences with other retired athletes. Exchange thoughts and feelings about the decision to retire and about adapting to a different lifestyle.
- If things are getting you down, discuss your concerns with someone close to you, or see a counselor for personal, educational, career, business, or leisure planning. Counselors are available on virtually all university campuses.

Positive Adaptation

What will happen to *you* when you move from a position of high acclaim (or at least recognition as an athlete) to what at first might appear to be nothing? If you sit around telling yourself that you are incapable of doing anything else, dwelling on how lousy things are, how great things used to be, or how the system screwed you, you will likely talk yourself into a state of depression. However, if you view this transition as an opportunity to grow in other areas, to expand, and to learn that the acclamation of others is simply not necessary for a rich and fulfilling life, then the passage will be much more positive.

If you have learned and perfected self-growth strategies while competing in your sport, you will take with you and have at your disposal one of the valuable contributions that sport can offer. This will ease your transition out of high-level competition and increase your chances of lifetime satisfaction.

As a retiring athlete, you still have most of your life ahead of you to direct as you please. It's not what's gone but what is left that counts. You can pursue all sorts of things that you were unable to do before, mainly because so much time and energy were concentrated on one focus. I never once skied in all those years I was competing in gymnastics. The seasons conflicted; besides, "you might get hurt." I discovered that I love skiing. You'll have ample opportunity to apply some of your sport psychology skills and focusing strategies to other meaningful pursuits. For example, goal setting, coping with stress, and refocusing can be readily transferred from sport to other areas. In addition, you will have much more time to spend with people you care about.

Some athletes do feel bitter and negative about their sports career after it is over. A few feel that as a result of all their striving, they have missed some important things in life, such as full involvement with their families, intimate relationships, enjoyable socialization with friends, or educational or occupational development. More often, athletes who leave with bitterness feel that they have been pawns, that they have been used or abused, then cast aside like garbage. People in their lives who had appeared to care so much in the past seemed quick to divert their attention elsewhere when the "machine" could no longer contribute to their ends.

It is true that certain people will use and abuse you for their own selfish ends. They may see you strictly as an object of performance, and when that object is no longer performing or following orders, it is of absolutely no value. This tells you more about those people than about yourself. Their insensitivity need not affect the way you see yourself as a person, unless you choose to accept their distorted view of humanity. Fortunately, a genuine sense of caring is shared by most athletes and coaches.

One way to strengthen your own position is to have input along the way. Make some choices for yourself. Establish your own goals. Then, in pursuing your goals, try to get the best out of your coach and yourself. Learn to understand your coach—how he sees the world—so you can better understand and utilize his strengths. If necessary, find another coach.

If upon retirement you start to get down on yourself for not being as good as you used to be, for going downhill physically, for being useless, and so on—think back. Think back to when you were a novice in your sport. You are a lot better now than you were then, in a lot of ways. Yet you were worthwhile then. Why should you be any less worthwhile now? A retired relationship can be viewed in a similar manner. Before you entered the relationship you were perfectly able to live and cope without the other person. You've grown over the years; you're more knowledgeable, more competent, more aware, and in some ways a better person. So why should you suddenly feel worthless and miserable? You are at least as worthy and as compassionate as you were in the past; besides, you have learned and gained from this experience.

If you need more legitimate self-support, remember that many people can't do anything as well as you can. Some people don't have their health; others are uncoordinated. Many do not even have their freedom. They are silenced by their governments or locked up in cages for a good portion of their lives. Shouldn't you be thankful for your relatively good health, your mental alertness, your coordination, your strengths, your freedom, your capacity to direct the rest of your life?

If you have gained from the experience itself, if it has contributed to your personal growth, if it has given you a sense of meaning (even temporarily), then it has been of some value. Draw upon this experience, and get on with developing other interests and other competencies. Prepare to open your own doors. Recognize that as one phase of your life is ending, another phase is just beginning.

Consider directing some of your hard-earned knowledge to the benefit of others by coaching a team, playing with a group of kids, giving clinics, or writing about your sport experiences. Your knowledge and contribution in your sport, and your understanding of people, can continue to grow throughout your life, long after your physical performance skills begin to decline. Or if you are sick of your sport, try something totally new for the sheer joy of doing it. What a beautiful feeling that can be after so many years of constant evaluation—as long as you can realign your performance expectations.

If you are overly concerned with performing well or with others' opinions, involvement in new activities may pose a problem. Some athletes (as well as nonathletes) are so afraid of looking less than perfect that they simply avoid anything in which they are not already proficient. If you have spent most of your time specializing in one activity, you may not be extremely proficient in others. Yet you can enjoy them immensely and can improve very rapidly once you make the step—once you realize that it doesn't really matter what others might expect from a former great in a certain sport. Who cares what the others think? Their thinking can't hurt you. You don't have to be a hero. You can be whoever you want to be. Just being you, with no pretenses, is fine.

"Most of our tensions and frustrations stem from compulsive needs to act the role of someone we are not. . . . 'Resolve to be thyself; and know that he who finds himself, loses his misery'" (Selye, 1956). Don't let anything get in the way of your growth and enjoyment. If you are not exceptionally proficient, others might even feel better and like you more. You are human just as they are—not great in everything.

An elderly woman who was preoccupied with the opinions of others had spent most of her life worrying and avoiding things. Her typical reflections were, Oh dear, what will people say? What will people think? What will people do if I do this or don't do that? She'd spend hours changing her clothes in the morning, worrying about what others might think if she wore one dress instead of another. A rather bizarre method was employed by a psychologist named Albert Ellis to convince the woman that others' opinions really made no difference. She was asked to wear a sandwich board while walking down a city street. On both front and back, the board read "I MESS AROUND." For the sake of the experiment she agreed to do it; much to her surprise, the world did not end. Most people didn't even notice, and the thoughts of those who did notice did not hurt her. It didn't really matter in the overall scheme. So what does it matter what others might think about which dress you wear or how well you play a new game? Perhaps there is a lesson in her story for the rest of us.

Developing Relationships

An athlete retiring from active competition often becomes more interested in establishing a meaningful and lasting primary relationship. For a variety of reasons this may not have been possible during the competitive years. Many highly committed amateur athletes do not date a great deal. Some do not ask; others are not asked; most simply do not have time. You may become classified as always away, always busy, unavailable, uninterested, untouchable, or a very important person.

Upon retirement you have more time to go after, or develop, what you want in a relationship. If you've been out of circulation, so to speak, you must somehow make yourself available to let a meaningful relationship develop, or place yourself in a position to meet interesting people.

Recreational or fitness settings provide a good opportunity to meet interesting people with similar interests. Active people seem to appreciate other active people. It's nice to share active pursuits. Sports clubs, fitness clubs, ski trails and slopes, parks, running trails, bicycle paths, fitness classes, canoe trips, evening courses, "fun" or self-paced competitions, conferences, leisure or hobby workshops, or pickup games can bring compatible and involved people together.

Meaningful relationships cannot be forced, but we all like to meet a compatible person to whom we are really attracted and who in turn treats us in a special way. Loving someone is a very special experience. If you are actively involved in doing things and in living, sooner or later you will meet other similar people who interest you. If you are genuinely interested in what someone says or does, and show it, that person is much more likely to show an interest in you. If you are friendly and receptive, others tend to reciprocate.

To develop sincere and intimate relationships, one of the most important, yet most difficult, tasks is to express our feelings openly to others. We spend much of our lives putting prophylactics over our emotions to hold everything in. This has a tendency to stifle relationships—if not in the short run, then certainly in the long run. If we don't know how a partner or prospective partner is feeling (or if the other person does not know how we are feeling), how can we adapt, adjust, or improve the situation? Saying what we feel in an honest and constructive way usually makes both partners feel better. It helps us to clarify our own feelings and values, lets others know where we stand, and strengthens the bond between people. Opening ourselves to intimacy can result in a beautiful experience, even though it makes us vulnerable at the same time.

The experience is worth the risk—and even the hurt, if that should occur. Life would be pretty boring if we refused to open our hearts, if we avoided all risk. Yes, sometimes there is risk; but there is more risk, over the long haul, in not expressing feelings. Communication on a feeling level is the basis for a fulfilling and lasting relationship.

Real intimacy in thoughts and feelings brings a deeper love, a more powerful bond. Intimacy shared with another person often yields intimacy in return. Tell a friend about a very personal feeling or problem, and your friend will almost always share something personal with you. That's the basis of intimacy. In the book *Discovering Your Hidden Self* (1976), Ann and Paul Frisch outline some good ways to foster a deeper, more personal, and more intimate connection between two people.

Mutual satisfaction in lovemaking also revolves around mutual consideration and open communication, not only physically but with respect to feelings. The two realms are interconnected, and the aim becomes heightened awareness and enjoyment for both partners. Lovemaking lends itself beautifully to full focus, followed by full relaxation, when approached in the right light.

Readers who would like more detailed information on retirement from sport should get a copy of *Athletes in Transition* (1987), which former Olympian Penny Werthner and I wrote specifically for retiring athletes.

Chapter 22

□

Closing in on Self-Direction

To live your life in your own way, to reach for the goals you have set for yourself, to be the you that you want to be—that is success.

The balanced pursuit of excellence is both demanding and fulfilling. Relish its intensity, cherish its beautiful moments, and accept its risks. Many lives lack this sense of intense absorption and personal meaning, the charged-up feeling, the flow of adrenalin, the body telling its master, I'm ready . . . let's go. This excitement is rarely duplicated elsewhere. Experience it and let it work for you.

Once we gain control of our inner world, competition need not be the fear trip that it has been for some people. Competition can be a unique opportunity to enhance performance, to be stimulated by others, to test self-control, to extend limits. Competitions can help you reach your goals. They can allow you to perform as you have never performed before. They can bring out your best. And even if they don't, there are lessons to be learned as you challenge yourself. When you keep sport in perspective, you can almost always emerge better from the experience.

Once you begin to view big games or important competitions in a positive light, you start to enjoy them more and look forward to them. The better you have prepared, the more confident you will likely feel during the competition. But once you are at the competition site, you have done everything that you can do. You might as well relax and enjoy the experience—and thereby free your body and mind to work for you. Most of us need the freedom from thoughts like "have to" or "should have" in order to deliver our best, most flowing performances.

If you find yourself questioning the value of your games or your life, it is often because you are currently failing to appreciate the good and satisfying things that you do have. Your focus on the negative pushes away the positive. The good is nonetheless there, though you momentarily turn your back on it. Why not open your heart to the good in life, to the value

within yourself, to the worth in others? Why not expand your appreciation to let the sun shine through during the bad times as well as the good
times? How else can you live life to the fullest?

When pursuing our life goals we must be careful not to fall into the
fatal trap that R.M. Pirsig describes in *Zen and the Art of Motorcycle
Maintenance* (1975, p. 206).

> He's here but he's not here. He rejects the here, is unhappy with it,
> wants to be further up the trail but when he gets there will be just
> as unhappy because he will be "here." What he's looking for, what
> he wants is all around him but he doesn't want that because it is all
> around him. Every step's an effort, both physically and spiritually,
> because he imagines his goal to be external and distant.

Wherever there is only a distant dream, a harsh reality is not far behind.
The real trip is in the experience, not necessarily in the arrival at a distant
destination. Unless you get immersed in your current experiences and
really enjoy them, dreams tend to remain dreams; worse yet, they explode
or fizzle away. All the more reason to become absorbed in this trip, as
well as many others.

As Leo Buscaglia points out in a book called *Love* (1972),

> There is only the moment. The now. Only what you are experienc-
> ing at this second is real. This does not mean, live for the moment.
> It means live the moment. A very different thing. . . . Live now. When
> you are eating, eat. When you are loving, love. When you are talk-
> ing to someone, talk. When you look at a flower, look. Catch the
> beauty of the moment.

As for change, it is inevitable. Feelings change, attitudes change, desires
change, people change, love changes. We can influence the direction of
change, but we cannot stop it, we cannot hold it back. Change directed
toward love and self-realization is always good.

Castaneda's Don Juan speaks of it in *The Teachings of Don Juan: A Yaqui
Way of Knowledge* (1974, p. 107).

> You must always keep in mind that a path is only a path. If you feel
> you must now follow it, you need not stay with it under any circum-
> stances. Any path is only a path. There is no affront to yourself or
> others in dropping it if that is what your heart tells you to do. But
> your decision to keep on the path or leave it must be free of fear and
> ambition. I warn you: Look at every path closely and deliberately.
> Try it as many times as you think necessary. Then ask yourself and
> yourself alone one question: Does this path have a heart? All paths

are the same. They lead nowhere. They are paths going through the brush or into the brush or under the brush. Does this path have a heart is the only question. If it does then the path is good . . . if it doesn't then it is of no use. Both paths lead nowhere, but one has a heart and the other doesn't. One makes for a joyful journey; as long as you follow it you will be one with it. The other will make you curse your life. One makes you strong, the other weakens you.

I used to think that the path to excellence was to work, work, work, shut out the rest of your life, and live only for the future. I was wrong! You do have to work extremely hard, but you don't have to shut out the rest of your life and you don't have to live *only* for the future. You can achieve the highest levels of excellence and still have a balanced and happy life in the here and now. This is the path to personal excellence, the path with a heart.

A renowned filmmaker and artist helped teach me this by example. When he works he becomes totally absorbed in his work, but he always leaves room for play. In fact, nothing—and I mean *nothing*—gets in the way of his play. His playtime enriches his life as much as any artistic achievement or outside honor bestowed upon him, probably more. It gives him something to look forward to with enthusiasm regularly, and it lets him return to his work with renewed energy.

He sets high goals and pursues them vigorously, but on a day-to-day basis he does not fail to appreciate his family, his own accomplishments, and the people around him. I love going to his house to ask if the "old man" can come out to play. He appreciates each experience so much that he's a delight to be with. His enthusiasm and vitality rub off on all those around him.

He used to accuse me jokingly of sitting at home writing books about having fun while he was out doing it. I reflected on the way he had come to keep playfulness at the center of a life that otherwise revolves around perfection and the pursuit of excellence. A near-fatal heart attack, which almost grabbed his life, helped teach him this lesson. He was thankful for another day of living . . . then another, and another. So many days to live and experience and enjoy. A gift of life!

Appendix

☐

Relaxation Exercise

This three-part relaxation exercise is designed to free you to enter a state of complete relaxation through muscle relaxation, relaxed breathing, and imagery.*

If you want to use the exercise to go to sleep, remind yourself before you begin listening that you will allow yourself to fall into a deep and restful sleep.

To use the exercise as a lead-in to performance imagery, remind yourself before you begin listening that at the conclusion of the exercise, while you are still in a deeply relaxed state, you will imagine and feel preselected performance skills flowing perfectly in your mind and body.

If you want to use the exercise to calm yourself before an important competition, select an appropriate time to listen—a time when you would prefer to be more relaxed and when you do not yet need to be highly activated for competing.

To use the exercise as a lead-in to strengthening your confidence, remind yourself before you listen that at the conclusion of the exercise you will repeat to yourself your many assets, your strengths, and your many reasons to be positive and confident in yourself and your capacity. You might want to write down some positive statements to think about before you begin the relaxation exercise.

If your objective is to heal your body or speed your recovery from a strenuous or stressful day, then prepare yourself to send healing thoughts and revitalizing images to various parts of your body—both during and after the relaxation exercise.

---

*Available on audiocassette, *In Pursuit of Personal Excellence*, from the Coaching Association of Canada, 1600 James Naismith Drive, Gloucester, ON: KIB 5N4 Canada.

Relaxation Script

Get yourself into a comfortable position. Let yourself relax. Feel the relaxation spread through your body. Breathe easily and slowly. Become aware of your feet. Move your toes slightly. Let them relax. Now think into your lower legs. Let your calf muscles totally relax. Think into your upper legs. Let them totally relax. Feel your legs sink into a completely relaxed state. Relax your behind. (Pause.)

Focus on the muscles in your lower back. Think relaxation into those muscles. Feel that relaxation spread into your upper back. Feel your whole body sink into a deep state of relaxation. Now focus on your fingers. Feel them tingle slightly. Think warmth into your fingers. Let them totally relax. Relax your forearms, your upper arms, and your shoulders. Totally relax. Relax your neck (pause) and your jaw. Feel your head sink into a totally relaxed and comfortable position.

Scan your body for possible areas of tightness and relax those areas. Feel your entire body encircled with soothing warmth and relaxation. Enjoy this wonderful state of complete relaxation.

(Pause 1 minute.)

Now focus on your breathing. Breathe easily and slowly.

(Pause.)

As you breathe in allow your stomach to rise and extend. As you breathe out let your whole body relax. Breathe in—feel your stomach rise. Breathe out—relax. Breathe in—feel your stomach rise. Breathe out—relax. (Do 3 times.) For the next 10 breaths, each time you breathe in feel your stomach rise—each time you breathe out think to yourself . . . relax . . . relax . . . relax (pause 10 breaths).

Feel yourself sink deeper and deeper into a calm and wonderful state of complete relaxation.

Now in your mind you are going to a very special place. You can go here whenever you want to find peace and tranquility. In your special place the sun is shining. The sky is blue. You are totally relaxed, enjoying the warmth and tranquility.

(Pause.)

Feel the warmth. Enjoy the beauty.

(Pause.)

You can be here alone or you can share this place with a special friend. It is your place. You decide.

In your special place, it is *so* relaxing. You are calm, relaxed, confident, and happy to be alive. You are in control. You feel great.

Feel the calmness spread through your entire body and mind as you rest gently, enjoying the peace and tranquility of your special place. You are feeling *so* good and *so* relaxed. You are comfortable, you are warm, you are safe. You are in control of your body and mind. Enjoy this wonderful, restful state.

References and Suggested Readings

Buscaglia, L. (1972). *Love.* Greenwich, CT: Fawcett.

Castaneda, C. (1974). *The teachings of Don Juan: A Yaqui way of knowledge.* New York: Pocket Books, Simon & Schuster.

Chapman, C., & Starkman, R. (1988). *On the edge: The inside story of the Canadian women's ski team.* Toronto: McGraw-Hill Ryerson.

Colgrove, M., Bloomfield, H., & McWilliams, P. (1976). *How to survive the loss of love.* New York: Bantam.

Ellis, A., & Harper, R.A. (1976). *A new guide to rational living.* North Hollywood, CA: Wilshire.

Frankl, V.E. (1968). *Man's search for meaning.* New York: Simon & Schuster.

Frisch, A., & Frisch, P. (1976). *Discovering your hidden self: Exercises in re-creative psychology.* New York: Signet.

Genge, R. (1976). Concentration. *Coaching Association of Canada Bulletin,* **12**, pp. 1-8.

Nideffer, R. (1976). *The inner athlete.* New York: Thomas Crowell.

Orlick, E.M. (1989). *How to rapidly and effectively hypnotize yourself.* Available from: Wizdom Enterprises, 16815 Milltown Landing Road, Brandywine, MD, 20613.

Orlick, E.M. (1989). *Hypnosis: The amazing speedway to sports success.* Available from: Wizdom Enterprises, 16815 Milltown Landing Road, Brandywine, MD, 20613.

Orlick, T. (1986). *Coaches training manual to* Psyching for Sport. Champaign, IL: Leisure Press.

Orlick, T. (1986). *Psyching for sport: Mental training for athletes.* Champaign, IL: Leisure Press.

Orlick, T., & Partington, J. (1986). *Psyched: Inner views of winning.* Gloucester, ON: Coaching Association of Canada.

Orlick, T., & Werthner, P. (1987). *Athletes in transition.* Gloucester, ON: Olympic Athlete Career Center/Coaching Association of Canada.

Otto, H. (1970). *Guide to developing your potential.* North Hollywood, CA: Wilshire.

Pirsig, R.M. (1975). *Zen and the art of motorcycle maintenance.* New York: Bantam.

Russell, B., & Branch, T. (1979). *Second wind.* New York: Ballantine.

Seligman, M. (1975). *Helplessness: On depression, development, & death.* San Francisco: W.H. Freeman.

Selye, H. (1956). *The stress of life.* New York: McGraw-Hill.

Suzuki, D.T. (1959). *Zen and Japanese culture.* New York: Pantheon, pp. 89-214.

Suzuki, D.T. (1971). In E. Herrigel, *Zen in the art of archery.* New York: Vintage, pp. v-ix.

Instructional Tapes on Mental Preparation

Botterill, C., & Orlick, T. (1988). *Visualization: What you see is what you get* [25-minute videotape]. Concerns the use of imagery by high-performance athletes. Available from the Coaching Association of Canada, 1600 James Naismith Drive, Gloucester, ON KIB 5N4 Canada.

Orlick, T. (1988). *In pursuit of personal excellence* [6-part audiocassette]. Includes elements of excellence, mental preparation for training, relaxation, refocusing, healing, and precompetition preparation. Available from the Coaching Association of Canada, 1600 James Naismith Drive, Gloucester, ON KIB 5N4 Canada.

□

Index

Other books by Terry Orlick

Every Kid Can Win, with Cal Botterill, 1975

The Cooperative Sports and Games Book, 1978

Winning Through Cooperation, 1978

The Second Cooperative Sports and Games Book, 1982

Mental Training for Coaches and Athletes, edited with John Partington and John Salmela, 1982

Sport in Perspective, edited with John Partington and John Salmela, 1982

New Paths to Sport Learning, edited with John Salmela and John Partington, 1982

Psyching for Sport: Mental Training for Athletes, 1986

Coaches Training Manual to Psyching for Sport, 1986

Psyched: Inner Views of Winning, with John Partington, 1986

Athletes in Transition, with Penny Werthner, 1987

Sharing Views on the Process of Effective Sportpsych Consulting, with John Partington, 1988

Nice on My Feelings: A Parent's Guide to Nurturing Children, 1990